FOUNDATIONAL STUDIES

Establishing Foundations

Aramis Torres

authorHOUSE®

AuthorHouse™
1663 Liberty Drive
Bloomington, IN 47403
www.authorhouse.com
Phone: 1-800-839-8640

First published by AuthorHouse 3/16/2010

ISBN: 978-1-4490-8346-5 (e)
ISBN: 978-1-4490-8345-8 (sc)

Library of Congress Control Number: 2010902628

Printed in the United States of America
Bloomington, Indiana

This book is printed on acid-free paper.

CONTENTS

Acknowledgments   vii

Foreword   xi

Introduction   1

Lessons

Lesson #1: Salvation   57

Lesson #2: Water Baptism   62

Lesson #3: The Holy Spirit   65

Lesson #4: Faith In God   68

Lesson #5: Jesus of Nazareth, The Messiah   70

Lesson #6: Prayer   73

Lesson #7: New Life In Christ   76

Lesson #8: The Bible   78

Lesson #9: ¿What Is Truth?   81

Lesson #10: The Family   84

Lesson #11: Continuing In Christ   87

Lesson #12: Communion and Congregation   89

Lesson #13: Fasting   91

Lesson #14: Giving & Receiving   93

Lesson# 15: The Church   95

Lesson #16: The Return of The King   97

Lesson #17: The New Covenant   99

Lesson #18: The Resurection of the Dead   102

Lesson #19: The Imposition of Hands   104

Lesson #20: Eternal Judgement   106

Lesson #21: The Christian Commandment - Love   108

<u>Appendices</u>

A1: The Head of the Church   111

A2: The Vision of the Church   115

A3: Gods Economy   119

A4: Faithfulness   122

A5: The Order of God   124

A6: Responsibility of the Church   126

A7: Confirmation   130

Our Covenant   133

Covenant of Confirmation*   135

References   137

Concluding Note   139

About the Author   141

ACKNOWLEDGMENTS

Before anything else, I want to thank the Almighty GOD for HIS*
Goodness, Grace, Love, and Mercy. Without a doubt, I have needed
all these diverse manifestations of GOD in my life. Thank you GOD
for your Son that died and shed His Blood for me, cleansing me from
all sin and unrighteousness. Thank you LORD for saving my soul, and
for Your HOLY SPIRIT, The Comforter that guides me, helps me,
and gives me testimony of Your Faithfulness. Thank you. Thank you.
Thank you.

It's almost impossible to remember all the names of people that over
the years have had such a powerful impact on my life and Christian
walk. I've tried to remember the names of as many as possible. If I
have forgotten someone, I ask for their forgiveness. GOD knows it has
not been on purpose. I thank GOD that HE does not forget, and HE
rewards all of those precious men and women, servants of GOD.

First, I want to thank GOD for my mom – Anelia Reyes Maldonado.
"Mami," although you are with The LORD, I want everyone here to
know of the great influence that as a mom you had in guiding and
encouraging your firstborn in the ways of The LORD. I will never forget
those eternal moments in which you challenged me to see who would
finish first in reading some of the books of the Bible, and later on to
see who could read the Bible, cover-to-cover first. Although I may have
claimed to win on those occasions, you were the one who really won,
for you got me to read the Bible everyone says they know but few have
read. I know that GOD will give you your reward mom, and we will
see each other again, just a little later.

---

*   *Masculine pronouns are used throughout this book, in order to describe The Almighty, but
technically speaking these are not applicable since our GOD is Spirit, and not man. Also the title
CHRIST is typically used to describe the Promised One, but the title Messiah could just as properly
be used.*

I also want to honor and thank my dad – Monserrate Torres Rivera, who GOD inspired to acquire his first Bible, as he desired to know more about GOD. I can still remember those days in which I would hear him call from one room to another "¡Anelia, ven aquí! ¡Mira lo que dice La Biblia (Anelia, come here! Look at what the Bible says!)," and how terrified she would be at the thoughts of excommunication that her religion threatened. As a devout woman, she had been raised in a religion that was interested in keeping her bound to the ignorance of tradition and ceremony.

Dad, I remember the efforts that you would make, to understand what was written in the Bible. I know it was GOD who inspired you to go beyond a religion that had no interest in you learning more. I'll never forget the barber that told you to go to a small church in a basement around the corner of his shop (on 87th Street), where they regularly studied the Bible. As I watched and listened, I learned in those days, the importance of diligently studying the word of GOD. Thanks dad for the transference of that meticulous study of the Bible.

I also want to thank GOD for those Christian brethren that are still living, as well as those that are already in heaven, for the spiritual and positive influences that they deposited in my life. I'll always remember: Rev. Hipólito Vega, Rev. Miguel Maldonado, Rev. Abelardo Berrios, Hno. Victor Muñoz, Rev. Miguel Salas, Rev. Frank Negron, Minister Serafín Velásquez, Rev. Tomas Santiago, Minister Valentín Cruz, Minister Luz Mercado, Rev. Bolívar Guadalupe, Minister Erminia and brother Echevarria of Sinai, Rev. Ventura and "Goyita" Hidalgo, Pastor Frank Macarone of Syracuse A.G., Rev. Emerito González Moya and Gloria Pagan, Rev. David López, Rev. T.L. Osborne, Brother Sixto Rivera, Rev. William Santiago, brother Ramón and his wife Petrin Torres, Rev. Israel DeJesus, Rev. Oscar Díaz, brother German and Carmen Cerezo, Rev. Benjamin Ocasio Sr., Rev. Tomas Pérez, Rev. Joaquín Maldonado, Rev. Rafael Reyes, Rev. George and Toni Peña, Rev. Samuel Chéverez Sr., Rev. Meléndez – missionary of Perú (whom GOD used powerfully to confirm the call of GOD upon my life), Sister Lucille Parella, Rev. Dr. Duran Palmertree, Rev. Antulio Rivera, Rev.

Aida DeJesus, Bishop John Gimenez, Rev. Jason Álvarez, Rev. Luciano Padilla, Rev. Emmanuel Canistraci, Rev. David Minor Sr. and Rev. Dr. Howard O. Jameson.

There are also a few more that I remember, but time has caused me to forget their names. LORD, I give you thanks because you don't forget them. Thank you LORD for that American evangelist, that parked his van on 91st Street in Manhattan, to minister to the children with his puppets. Thank you LORD for that ministry touched my life. Thank you LORD for the evangelist from England, that my wife and I met on the day that we were having our first home service at my mom's house in New York City. I thank you LORD for using this English evangelist as your instrument, so that my daughter at five years old could understand and make the decision to accept Jesus as her Savior in 1984. Thank you LORD.

Almighty GOD, I also thank you for Dr. Greenberg, the Jewish principal of my elementary school. Thank you for his friendship and vision. I also thank you for inspiring him to take me to the synagogue he attended, so that I could know and participate in some of the customs and celebrations of YOUR PEOPLE the Jewish people. Thank you LORD. I ask that YOU bless your people Israel, and that YOU Bring peace to the land of Israel. Also, I ask that YOU continue to individually bless and prosper YOUR PEOPLE, who are still dispersed throughout the world. Thank you LORD, for they are truly a blessing that YOU have given to all the nations. May they soon receive their visible Messiah, the Son of David, so that in turn the world will also finally know PEACE as HE rules as KING from Israel - The BLESSED ONE whose Kingdom is FOREVER. I also thank you for ALL my Jewish friends. May they get to know the peace that is available to them through a relationship with YOU. Again I ask LORD, Bless them!

Finally, I thank my wife, Rebecca for being my friend, my helper, my lover, my nurse, the mother of my beautiful children, the intercessor in my house and my life-long companion. I want you to know that I appreciate all of your prayers, your help, your support, your love, and your continual faithfulness to GOD and to myself. I thank you sweetheart, for choosing to love me even during those times when I have been difficult to love.

Rev. Aramis Torres, DD
Senior Pastor
La Roca Church of Sussex County

FOREWORD

Dr. Aramis Torres is an accomplished theologian and Bible scholar. The material in this book reflects a lifetime of study and preparation.

With uncanny perception, Dr. Aramis has focused on the salient issues in this area of biblical inquiry. With the deft skill of a master craftsman, he has broken down difficult concepts so the novice can understand the material and benefit from it both intellectually and spiritually.

As you begin your journey through this book, allow the HOLY SPIRIT to minister to you. You are about to undergo a change and a growth process. For this, we thank GOD. May the benefit you derive from this study not only bless you, but may it enable you to be a blessing to others as you share these truths.

Howard O. Jameson, Ph.D.
Jameson Schools of Ministry and
Theology, Philadelphia, PA

INTRODUCTION

Over the years GOD has allowed me to walk a path that I'm the first to admit has given me the opportunity to meet so many wonderful people, at various stages of human development, maturity and understanding, in the Christian world. Of course when I say this, I'm including the place where every Christian goes to: Church. Without a doubt in the course of my life I have visited many Christian churches, particularly here in the USA, with their variety of customs, traditions, and teachings.

As a little boy I became aware that the religion of my parents, was the Roman Catholic Church with all of its' great temples, beautiful ceremonies and traditions. Every time we went, I would sit down and admire the buildings - stately, silent, and impressive. GOD had to be there. Many years later I was introduced to the Pentecostal church with it's' vibrant energy and life in the Spirit. As time went on, I also encountered other churches and traditions. These ran the gamut of the old line Protestant churches (Baptist, Methodist, Presbyterian, etc) to the newer Charismatic Catholic churches, as well as various Christian congregations with very unique traditions (those with the veils, the Seventh Day Adventists, Jesus only, church of prophecy, etc.).

As the years went by, I had the privilege of meeting and speaking with a variety of people from different congregations. While I was still too young to be taken seriously by many, I was able to listen in to the conversations people had with my dad, as they explored their faith and discovered more of the Bible. As time progressed, I was able to understand that these individuals represented a small microcosm of the Church of Jesus Christ with its personal; spiritual and secular outlook. I came to understand that from the richest to the poorest, from the most educated to the least educated, there are things that we absorb, that make us unique and slightly different in our ecclesiastical and personal views of the GOD of the Bible. Why? I began to wonder. Interestingly

1

I have found that the various manifestations of the Church of Christ that I've encountered in the USA, Canada, Puerto Rico, and Cuba, are all very similar but with the unique flavor that represents the array of experiences and outlooks that their members have had.

What a beautiful thing is the Church of Jesus Christ. There is such a variety of personal experiences that people have with GOD, along with their accompanying growth and maturity as there are people in the churches! After more than 40 years in the church I've had the privilege to speak with such a beautiful array of people from various cultures and ethnic backgrounds that have been impacted by the many Christian churches and traditions previously mentioned, that there is no doubt GOD is in the Church. I believe that it has been the plan of GOD for me to sit and listen to such an array of precious brethren as they shared their various and unique experiences in their search and encounters with GOD. What a privilege!

In the conversations I've had with so many wonderful Christians, I've been able to discover that the vast majority of these people (because of their love of GOD0, have been able to acquire wisdom and maturity that truly comes from GOD. I've been personally blessed to understand that GOD works through people, even among those that I wouldn't normally expect.

Over the years, some of these precious brethren have told me about some of the adventures they had in their Christian walk. I also got to hear of the difficulties and afflictions that they suffered, as well as the many errors that they committed, until they finally began to understand by the HOLY SPIRIT, the plan of GOD for their lives.

As a child, I heard many elderly people use the expression "I've had to pay the price," as they described their experiences and current effectiveness in Christ. Now, I realize that this was something that I did not fully comprehend until much later on as an adult. Once again, I have to say, "Thank you LORD." On this occasion, it is for the growth that GOD gives HIS children, despite what some leaders may have taught or didn't teach.

It seems to me, that too often some of our leaders have been negligent in teaching what I call the "full counsel of GOD" (a balanced view and teaching of the Bible – from Genesis to Revelation). Perhaps I'm giving them the "benefit of the doubt" when I say it probably was not on purpose. Maybe it was because many of them had not been taught completely by their own leaders and teachers, when they first began their walk. In any case, I thank GOD for HIS continual help and guidance of the Church of JESUS CHRIST. We have needed it.

It is my belief, that all of us have to go through a personal school of the HOLY SPIRIT. In fact, it is my opinion that if you truly love GOD, the less you know of the Scriptures the more of GOD'S intervention you will need. It is my hope and belief that GOD will not allow any of his children to grow-up twisted or malformed, for that is not the will of GOD. Of course I'm not including everyone, just those that truly love GOD. There are those that only have a "form of godliness" (which I'm using here to mean that they "attend the church" but only for the benefits – just like the seats or chairs that are being sheltered from the elements) but without "paying the price" or the cost of being faithful to GOD and HIS WORD. Yes, that does include giving your offerings and tithes. Yes, it means that you are PART of a congregation that will help those in need – first in the congregation, then those in the community that we are commanded to help – the widows and the orphans. The Apostle John declares very bluntly *"In this the children of God and the children of the devil are manifest: Whoever does not practice righteousness is not of God, nor is he who does not love his brother."* 1John 3:10

I also remember my religious history studies in High School. It was only after a few months of study that I began to think that perhaps religion was an invention of the devil (I can now include "the flesh" since man can be horribly cruel also). It didn't take too long to understand that religion was not invented by THE REAL GOD. After all, what type of god needs to have people punished on their behalf? Are these gods unable to defend their own positions? Are these gods too weak or too far away to take care of their own issues? Oh yeah, it's the MPD gods (the mute, paraplegic and deaf gods). They have mouths, but cannot

3

speak and ears but cannot hear, they have hands but cannot touch, etc. It was in that history class that I found out about the millions of people that have been killed by religious fanatics across the world. Unfortunately, I also found out that I had to include many of the leaders of my Catholic background to this group of terror. Yes there were the usual deluded and violent civilizations and religious fanatics that I had come to expect from world history – Aztecs, Druids, Baal worshippers, Mayans, Muslims, etc., but now I could not gloss over the fact that it also included a "mainstream" Christian religion! Although mostly led by the Roman Catholic hierarchy, it was guilty (the rest of the people were kept ignorant, docile, and afraid) of mass murder! Now I won't ignore that although on an extremely smaller scale, evangelicals also got into the act. The bottom line is that all of them acted in their own self-righteousness, and interest, BUT IT WAS NOT IN THE RIGHTEOUSNESS OF GOD.

CHRISTIANS – we are COMMANDED to LOVE OUR NEIGHBOR! We are not commanded to kill them or abuse them! When I studied *Dante's Inferno*, in school, I could also visualize the deepest, hottest spots in hell as especially set aside for all the selfish, violent, and misguided fanatics in history like Attila and his hordes, Genghis Khan and his hordes, Mohammed and his bands, the propagators of the Spanish Inquisition, Hitler and his madmen, as well as many others that history records their fanaticism and cruelty. As an educated young man, I realized that I had to include people from my religious faith in this group of violent people. The beautifully dressed Popes directing the Crusades, the stately Cardinals and Bishops who continued to propagate the lies of the inquisition and their religious fanaticism (e.g., Bishop and later as Cardinal Carafa – then later on as Pope Paul IV), as well as the other despots of the Roman church that preceded him. This wasn't a campaign against evil people, for even simple priests and ministers were also killed for daring to read, think and discuss what the scriptures really said. I recommend a book that may now be out of print "Foxes Book of Martyrs" (you may want to check your local library or look for any local bookstores that specialize in old books). Yes it does bring out a lot of "dirty laundry" but we ALL need to clean our stuff from time to time.

Unfortunately, too many of our religious leaders, come across as outright liars because of their alignment with religions that have historically hidden the truth from their congregants or used traditions invented by themselves, to cloud the truth that should be evident to all! Many of these same leaders are and were among the ones who introduced the vicious poison of "anti-Semitism" to the Church of JESUS CHRIST, and who even to this day still want to defend their antecedent's historical stance. Hello, Hello? All you anti-Semites in case you didn't know it, the Lord Jesus Christ was born Jewish! Hello? Hello? Is anybody listening? The zealous Christian Apostle Paul was even willing to die for his JEWISH people, so that they would believe his gospel. Wait. Why go to Paul? Let's go directly to the source - Jesus the Jewish Rabbi, who <u>did die</u> for His Jewish brethren FIRST, but included everyone else!

As Christians we need to reject every poisonous word that we hear about our JEWISH brethren. That's right OUR JEWISH BRETHREN, not just our Christian brethren. Please realize this: we weren't grafted into a "Christian" tree, or made partakers of a "Christian Israel." No! We are grafted into the tree of Abraham, Isaac, and Jacob! By faith we are also Abraham's seed. We Christians are hoping and waiting for the Kingdom of the "Son of David." We want to be partakers of the Kingdom of the Jewish Messiah. As I jokingly tell my Jewish friends from time to time, "When are you guys going to setup your Empire?" The world needs it. Needs what? To be saved from itself! Jesus said in John 4:22 *"We know what we worship: for salvation is of the Jews."* Again, let us <u>REJECT ALL ANTI-SEMITISM</u>.

I'm so glad that all the rest of us folks (the non-Popes, non-Cardinals, non-Bishops, etc), who are not power hungry or interested in keeping some historic control of "whatever," can depend completely on what the Scripture says in Philippians 1:6, *"HE who has begun a good work in you will complete it until the day of Jesus Christ."* Thank you GOD. We are here to serve YOU, and to cherish ALL YOUR people. As one of my favorite Bible verses says, *"we know that we have passed from death to life, because we love the brethren."* 1 John 3:14

If I go back a few years (before I went to high school), as I got closer to my teenage years, I encountered some devious and carnal teachings that began to stealthily enslave me. It was religion disguised as GOD. Although many people mean well in the Kingdom of GOD, they forget that anything that is not led by the Spirit of GOD, is NOT from GOD. During that time, I encountered "reasonable" people that taught me "Don't do this" or don't do that" in order to please GOD. Although these things seemed reasonable, since they seemed to be backed up with a variety of scriptural verses, these teachings were designed (by the devil) to bind my intellect and enslave me. Without realizing it, I began to think that serving GOD was an issue of "what I had to do," and NOT what "HE had already done." It didn't matter that by then, I had already read the Bible completely from cover to cover at least twice. Everything I knew until then was due to intellectual effort without "practical" experience. At that point in my life, I had already graduated from a Bible correspondence school (at about ten years old), and had faithfully attended every Sunday school class that was given during the previous three years. Yes, I had already run into a few things that seemed to contradict each other, but my "ready" acceptance of what the people I admired said, allowed me to ignore what my instincts were telling me. I had already been taught that the New Testament was designed to replace the Old Testament (what a devious lie that is!), and that the Church had replaced Israel, for we had a "better" covenant. Instinctively I could not understand this reasoning, since it required that I accept that a PERFECT GOD had somehow changed HIS mind over the years, but at that time I didn't pursue it any further.

It was during this time that my parents became interested in further Bible study, and began to attend the Bible institute of the Latin American Council of Spanish Churches, held at the place known as "La Sinagoga." Since I wasn't allowed to stay at home (I was too young), I had to accompany my parents to "La Sinagoga" (in order for my parents to attend the school they had gotten permission to have me sit quietly next to them as they were at class).

As my parents attended school (at the time directed by Rev. Abelardo Berrios, Esq.), I sat "quiet as a mouse" while classes were being taught.

Since both my parents eventually graduated from this school, although at different times, I accompanied both of them. My dad went for three years and then my mom went for three years. Without knowing it, GOD had already set HIS plan for my life into motion. Although officially I was not a student, I'm sure that very few people noticed that the skinny little kid sitting quietly near his dad or his mom was not asleep or busy playing, as might be expected. I know that very few if any, realized that this young boy was sitting there listening attentively to the teachers that were directing the classes at the time. Typically, when we went home, I would even borrow the school books from my parents, so as to read them on my own, and clarify some question I had. My favorite book at the time was a book entitled *Systematic Bible Theology* (*Teología Bíblica y Sistemática*) by Meyer Perlman (I didn't even have to search for the title or the author's name, since it's still vividly inscribed in my memory).

A few years ago, after attending a funeral of an elderly person I had known as a kid, I asked my dad if he knew anything about the current state of a particular individual (Rev. Salas), who was a teacher for one of the classes my dad and later on my mom, took in their second year. My dad was shocked and asked how it was possible that I still remembered that person? I answered him and said that this teacher was one of my favorites at "La Sinagoga," back when they were attending classes, over forty years ago! Although my dad had forgotten, I reminded him that I attended class for three years with my mom and for three years to almost every single class that he had also gone to at the time.

As I look back, I realize that my voracious appetite for reading (thanks Mom for encouraging it), along with my curiosity about almost everything, when applied to what was written in the Bible, caused me to remember the stories and much of the data that is in the Bible, to this day. Further, since the Churches I attended at the time also had the equivalent of "Bible Olympics" (memory competitions) every year, I had memorized sufficient chapters of the Bible so as to win all potential contests of Scripture memorization that I might have been allowed to participate in. Unfortunately, I was not allowed to compete with the adult contestants, but I knew as a kid, that I could easily beat almost all of them, without working up a sweat. This knowledge was already puffing me up. Later on in my Christian life, I came to understand 2 Corinthians 3:6, that it was the letter that kills, but the Spirit gives life.

Despite my memorization ability, it took a few years for me to discover that somehow, unbeknownst to me, I had fallen for lies disguised in religious jargon, and that these had bound me. It was after going through the process that I had to go through, that I began to understand that it was the SPIRIT of GOD whom I had been missing. My intellect, without the HOLY SPIRIT, was unable to quickly expose the insidious lies that religion, disguised as GOD, had given me. When I began to truly seek "the beloved," was when I found the Word of Life. Even now I remember parts of a song from my childhood, "Jesus llego, salio el poder maligno.." (Jesus arrived and the evil power left).

I can say without a doubt that the Spirit of GOD is the One who builds and leads the Church of Christ! The church of Jesus Christ is not a specific denomination or a specific Council or a specific congregation. The Church of Christ is the individual that has been born again, that loves GOD with all their heart, with their entire mind, and with all their strength. These are the ones that even when there has been a lack of proper instruction by a teacher, or a Pastor, are somehow prepared supernaturally by the HOLY SPIRIT in the word of GOD, for they have allowed GOD to change their hearts as He desires.

Now in this generation, in these "last days," we need to go beyond our daily circumstances, or our denominational affiliations. GOD does what He said He would do, but we have to do what we're supposed to do. Romans 10:14 says, *"How then shall they call on him in whom they have not believed? And how shall they believe in him of whom they have not heard?"* We need to let everyone know that GOD is interested in us. HE created us for HIS purposes. We cannot be complete without HIM. In our inner man, there is a space that can only be filled by GOD. Every human being wonders, "Why am I here?" and also, "Does my life really matter?" Once we encounter the Creator, it is by HIS HOLY SPIRIT, that those questions are answered.

As I was saying earlier, in many of the conversations that I have had over the years with other Christians, the LORD has allowed me to hear ideas regarding some of the aspects of the Word of GOD, which have demonstrated to me that these people have not been taught what the Scriptures say. Many have not received or understood what "the whole counsel of GOD is." Too often these people have had to learn in the "school of hard-knocks," as the old cliché goes, in order to develop into the genuine followers of JESUS CHRIST.

Unfortunately many of my fellow Christians have not been instructed in some of the most basic Bible doctrines by their mentors and teachers. Many of them, have had to wait years before they finally heard someone highlight what should have been one of the basic teachings that they learned at the beginning of their Christian walk. Now, the question is "who should have explained to them, exactly what the Bible says?" Should it have been: their pastor, their priest, their minister, or their Sunday school teacher? On occasion I've seen people react with anger and irritation towards their particular denomination, and a few of them even towards their pastors, upon hearing and reading what the Bible really says. Well, whose fault is it? It's not GOD. I also think that for the most part, it's not even the fault of the Pastors or Teachers. I'm not going to say that they're completely innocent, just that the brunt of the responsibility is not theirs alone! Yes, they should have at least taught the people how to study, and perhaps they should have assigned some Bible sections for people to read and meditate upon, but there's still room for plenty of blame to go around. Who is at fault then? 2 Timothy 2:15 says, *"Be diligent to present yourself approved to GOD, a worker who does not need to be ashamed, rightly dividing the word of truth."* Putting that into today's vernacular, this simply means "It's your responsibility."

I'm sure that most of the "loose ends" in the kingdom happen because of the overall lack of importance that has been assigned to personal study of the Bible. Since many of us have come from a Roman Catholic background, perhaps it's the laziness transmitted by the Roman hierarchy that we don't need to make effort because that is why they are there. Today I'd even add that it's also possibly caused or reinforced by the superficial comments and quick overviews that continue to be paraded all around us by the cable and TV media, via a variety of celebrity Bible Scholars (University Professors, ministers, and other seemingly prepared or well-intentioned individuals). I would point to the beautifully orchestrated and generated publicity (by historians, professors, ministers, publishers, archeologists, etc.) for Dan Browns blockbuster book *"The DaVinci Code,"* as an example. Most conversations about this book of fiction were all about things that really are fiction.

Now, I've noticed that some Biblical "oversights" that have occurred, are probably more obvious in congregations that seem to "specialize" in certain areas that their congregation or denomination emphasizes or is known for. However, over the years the observations that I have made, have made me very sad. There is a general lack of cohesive Biblical knowledge among most of the people in our churches. In fact, it's most distressing to me to hear "Christian" people often quote things that they have heard from poorly informed individuals, as if these things were actually written or supported in the Bible!

I have also noticed, when I've taken the time to watch a supposed "history" or "documentary" type film, that some very obvious errors are promulgated as fact, when ordinarily this would not occur if people would just read what they're talking about, and then place what they've read in the context that it occurs! The lack of scholarship that is evident (no not the genuine university research that has taken place, but the lack of actual literal reading of the Scriptures by many of the commentators) is downright embarrassing. If it were not that we are talking about the Word of the Living GOD, it would almost be hilarious. One expert quotes another expert, who quotes another expert, who quotes another expert...etc. and these experts have not even bothered to read the passages in question! Sadly, many times when Christians get thrown into the mix, they themselves repeat things that they <u>should know contradicts what is written</u>, and which they should know in their heart, can't be right.

At the risk of excessive use of generalizations, I think that another issue affecting the Christian church is that too many people in the churches have been working with an empty "mission plan." What do I mean by this? They are not doing what the GOD of the Bible teaches. For example: Success is measured here in the USA by the size of a congregation; the amount of money that comes in or that goes out; the popularity of the ministers; by the number of people that their TV/Radio programs reach; by the type of car that they drive; or by the political clout that they wield, and not by their adherence to the teachings of the Master – Jesus of Nazareth.

Here we are in the 21st Century. Almost everything seems to be available to the ministers and their congregations. It's like never before. Almost everyone in ministry is familiar with the various workshops/seminars that are available throughout the year via: the internet, radio and television, the Colleges, Universities, and the Seminaries around us. We have almost everything readily available at our fingertips. We have: church growth seminars, building expansion strategies, ministry outreach programs, accounting technologies, sermon preparation software, technology for our song services, funding seminars to increase our income, money management courses, and on and on. I have no doubt that this is the day that we should reach the world for Christ!

Now, please don't misunderstand me if I come across a little negative now, for I don't mean to. All these things that I've listed are not bad in and of themselves; it's just that IT IS NOT what the Church needs. What we really need NOW (I'm reminded of the old song "What the world needs now, is love sweet love...") is to find out how WE CAN BEST PLEASE GOD. HE is the source of all THAT IS PERFECT, or as the Bible describes it in James 1:17 *"Every GOOD gift and every PERFECT gift is from above, and comes from the Father of lights, with whom there is no variation or shadow of turning"* and HE want us to encounter this perfect gift of love that has been given to us. I'm also reminded of another verse that I would hear at most evangelical churches when I was a kid: James 4:10 *"Humble yourselves in the sight of the Lord, and HE will lift you up."* Additionally, I remember the words of the prophet Zechariah, still sung or quoted by Jews in their synagogues throughout the world, it's Zechariah 4:6 *"Not by might nor by power, but by My Spirit says The Lord."* I truly believe that it is time for us to move away from our wonderful ideas and plans, and look towards GOD for the true and perfect direction that HE will provide.

Let's change the way we currently do things. Let us go back to some of the "old ways" still practiced by some of our Jewish brethren throughout the world, as well as by the persecuted Church throughout the world. Every day, let's set time aside to read or meditate on the book that GOD has given us – The Bible. Let's not focus on reading ten chapters or perhaps one book every day, or whatever. Let's pick no more than a chapter at a time, or a few verses at a time, and meditate upon what we've read. Let's make the decision to read the Bible in context. Perhaps you can pick a specific day during the week, where you can read as much as you'd like, but choose all the other times to read the Scripture with reverence and with care, asking GOD to help you understand what you've read.

In my ministry experience, I have seen that it is the lack of consistent, purposeful, planned study and/or teaching coupled with prayer that has so many people in the churches bound and weak. Bound to what? People are bound to a life of: insufficiency, questions without answers, few victories, few miracles, and weak with their lack of GOD'S power. What then should our focus be in our churches? Our congregations don't need another revival meeting. We don't need internationally renowned minister "so and so" to come and enthrall us with their skillful preaching or enticing charisma. We don't need any more church growth plans. The only thing we need is to ENCOURAGE ONE ANOTHER TO TRULY KNOW CHRIST! Without a doubt, it's time that the leaders of all the churches teach the same thing, preach the same thing, and live the same thing. The Bible says, "Jesus Christ is the same yesterday today and forever," but what has happened to us? This has to become more than a motto of our churches. We need to have it as a style of life that causes Jesus Christ to be real in each and every one of us - from the youngest to the oldest.

Beloved, it is time to truly demonstrate the GOD of the Bible in all our congregations, as well as to the world. This is not hard, if we make the decision today, to build the Kingdom of GOD as the Lord wants and not as we want. Let's not imitate the disciple Peter who in a moment of jealousy asked in John 21:21 *"what about this one (speaking about the disciple John)?"* It doesn't matter who is around us but we need to resist the ideas and the temptations that come from the pit of hell (that's jealousy, envy, covetousness, etc.), no matter how popular or fashionable these ideas may be. We don't want to imitate those that demonstrate weaknesses and prejudices, as they try to build their own kingdoms. NO. We want to imitate CHRIST.

The disciple John, along with others, perhaps under pressure to conform to the "cool group" known as the disciples of Rabbi Jesus, also committed a similar error to what Peter had succumbed to. Mark 9:38 *"Teacher, we saw someone who does not follow us casting out demons in your name, and we forbade him because he does not follow us."* When I read this it sounds so much like the words spewing out of too many of the leaders of our councils, our churches, and the media of this day. It boils down to disciple against disciple. "Watch out they're not one of us!" "Stay away from those crazies," for they are "against this" or they are "intolerant of that." Without a doubt, we have to change our ways.

Today is the day to reflect Jesus. Let's all speak what the Lord wants - that which we all know, that which we are all in agreement that the Bible says: the good news that GOD loves you, and that He has provided the manner in which you can reach him. Let's teach and preach: that He will clean and wash us of all of our sins; that He loves us; that He will never leave nor forsake us; that when He thinks about us He thinks only the best about us. We need to teach that He wants us to prosper in everything; He wants to talk to us; He wants us to seek Him; that He will help us to be like Christ; that He wants to fill us with his Spirit; and that Jesus is coming back for us.

Oh course when I say we should speak the same thing and teach the same thing, I'm not including the few things where we do have some genuine differences of opinion amongst ourselves as Christians. There are a few things in the Bible that the Lord does not give us enough data to form a specific teaching on. For example when is really the return of Jesus? This has been asked since the days in which Jesus walked on the earth with his disciples! The Lord did give us a few signs that have to take place before his return, but they are very general and not easily assigned to a specific day or month or year. Until certain things finally do occur, for example - where the prophet Daniel actually gave an actual number of days after the start of the daily sacrifices, no one knows the day or the hour of His return.

In cases where there exist various theories and opinions, I counsel everyone to take the position that GOD permits us to take - speak the truth that we do know. If we have to respond to something that we as yet do not know or understand, or if we're aware that there are disagreements in this specific area among Christians, the easiest thing to do is to send these people with questions to your pastor or the assigned teachers in your congregation. Now, if circumstances do not permit this, then we need to indicate very clearly that whatever we are going to express is an opinion of ours (if we have one). Learn to say, "Although the Bible is not clear in this area, in MY OPINION, and I emphasize that it is my opinion, I think the following may be..."

Look, when the Bible does not specify the things that are necessary for us to form a solid doctrine (teaching), we shouldn't allow our ego (or our pride) to interfere and lead us into error.

Don't propagate your opinions. Be especially careful if you think that by expressing your opinion: you may sound more intelligent or wiser than others, or if you think that it will cause other people to know that you have much more revelation than anyone else. This is not from GOD! On the contrary, using the example I gave previously - regarding the return of Jesus Christ - instead of insisting that your position or belief is absolutely correct, stand in the position that most pleases GOD - humbleness. All of us know that he is coming, and therefore let us teach what we don't argue about - He is coming and we need to be ready! Amen.

Generally speaking there seems to be a lack of consistency in the basic doctrines of the Bible that we should all have in this day of such advances in knowledge, technology, and general sciences. There is no excuse for us to <u>disseminate ideas or opinions</u> that common sense and science indicate to us are false. We need to cast aside those questions and teachings that are tempting and carnal but which divide us. This is not from GOD. The Bible tells us "GOD is one." Let us therefore ALSO reflect that oneness or unity that is GOD. If we give ourselves to the Word and the direction of the HOLY SPIRIT, we will begin to answer those foolish and tempting questions that too often arise, with the sharp truth of The Word of GOD.

It's amazing the number of times that I have found myself with Christians, who are still wondering about questions that should seem ridiculous and foolish to them by now! Please understand me, I don't mean to say that they are ridiculous or foolish; instead it is that these people truly do not have a solid biblical foundation, and that is why they wonder about such silly things. Of course there is always the possibility that they are trying to accommodate teachings that their leaders (or denomination) have promoted, combined with ideas that they have read or heard elsewhere. For example:

- Are the gifts of the HOLY SPIRIT for today or not?

How sad. There are leaders today teaching an abbreviated form of the great commission, found in Mark 16:15-18, where Jesus said, *"Go ye into all the world, and preach the gospel to every creature. He that believeth and is baptized shall be saved; but he that believeth not shall be damned. And these signs shall follow them that believe; in my name shall they cast out devils; they shall speak with new tongues; they shall take up serpents; and if they drink any deadly thing, it shall not hurt them; they shall lay hands on the sick, and they shall recover."*

What some of these leaders are saying, are adjustments to what the Bible actually teaches. Seemingly they do not read the same things that you and I read; instead they propose adjustments like "this last part is only for the apostles, and the early church. It is not for us today." Wait a minute; all the translations I've read to date, do not have these types of "adjustments." I ask for your forgiveness first, as I sarcastically make the following comment: perhaps these teachers and ministers have discovered a lost manuscript where Jesus actually says, "after hundreds of years my name will lose its power" or "this was only for the church in Jerusalem…." How ridiculous this is. Either we accept what is written as "gospel" or when we reject part of what it says, we are agreeing with the current anti-Christ, anti-Bible, anti-GOD spirit of these "last days." Imagine that. These teachers and ministers are agreeing that the Bible is a compendium of false ideas, unable to help mankind or its' human condition. HELLO! It's best if you went back to school and took up house-painting as a career!

I have no doubt that in a world full of relativism, puffed up with doubt and unbelief; we need today a demonstration of the power of GOD, as never before. I believe that this can only happen, when we RAISE THE LEVEL OF THE BIBLE to that of THE INERRANT, UNCOMPROMISED WORD OF THE ALMIGHTY GOD!

- These gifts, do they come from the spirit of GOD or do these gifts need to be learned in school?

This is another of the common but seemingly useless questions that imply that GOD is limited in human affairs. Are you able to move GOD aside because you are now god? Is it possible that you no longer need the help of GOD because you are completely self-sufficient? Without too much doubt, it is possible that you can potentially learn many of the languages of the world just by going to school. BUT, is this what is required in order for you to be used by GOD? As we look at the various schools/seminaries and ministries that perhaps unknowingly limit GOD (e.g., in order to be used by GOD you have to be a seminary school graduate, or in order to speak in tongues it means you went to a school to learn different languages). If GOD is the Almighty GOD, then all these individuals must be serving a different god because the GOD and Father of Jesus Christ could supernaturally empower the disciples in Acts chapter 2 to speak in languages that they had not studied!
Back in the eighties, I heard a Presbyterian minister testify over the radio in Dallas Texas, "one of the elderly members of our church stood up, while I was preaching, and uttered something in another language interrupting my sermon! As soon as he quieted down, I was so upset

that I quickly concluded my sermon. Almost as an afterthought I asked if anyone wanted to come and receive Jesus as Savior. A young man visiting from college came forward. At the end of the service, I asked the young man who had came forward to receive Christ as his savior what part of the message I preached touched him, and he replied <u>none!</u> It was the old man who had spoken so beautifully in this young mans native language, telling him that he needed to serve Jesus!"

- Does GOD heal today or is this something of the past?

Here we have some more limitations. I remember reading the story of Elijah, when he spoke to the prophets of Baal, "shout louder, for Baal may be busy." When Jesus died, did His GOD and Father stop being GOD? Should a prophet of Baal come and goad us, telling us to "shout louder because GOD is busy?" Is GOD really so busy, that what his Son said to us no longer applies? What foolishness! The PROBLEM WE HAVE today, even as it was yesterday, is LACK OF FAITH in GOD.

- Are miracles, no longer from GOD but a deception of the devil for these days?

If Jesus is lifted up before men, by miracles and signs and wonders confirming His word, and we dare to say that this is the devil, we commit some very grievous errors: First, we forget what Jesus himself said, *"These signs shall follow..."* Second, Jesus also said in Mark 3:24, *"a kingdom divided against itself cannot stand."* Third, Jesus said in John 10:10, *"The thief does not come except to steal, and to kill and to destroy..."* These foolish individuals are declaring JESUS is a liar, for what HE said is not true. And finally, fourth - they are blaspheming the HOLY SPIRIT, by assigning the work of GOD to the devil! Amazingly to me, as I was driving one day listening to the radio, I heard the elderly president of a chain of Christian radio stations; actually deride a caller who wanted to know about miracles for today! He declared that these were signs designed to fool "even the elect!" What craziness! The ACTUAL physical anti-Christ has not been manifested as yet, but any healings are attributed to this deceiver already? How can individuals like this, or churches, or even ecclesiastical councils, actually suggest that it is the devil that is operating miracles in the name of Jesus, so as

17

to fool people! HOW is this? I have yet to hear about any minister or evangelist or pastor, or miracle worker – do something in the Name of Jesus, and then declare themselves or their ideas as the proof that Jesus was not the Son of God!? What insane foolishness.

Wait one moment. Come on, pick up your brain, and use it for a moment. Don't we agree that the new birth is a miracle of GOD? If we follow the logic of these foolish teachers and leaders, and we agree with their false premise, we must also say, "Miracles are not for today, therefore you CANNOT BE BORN AGAIN. You have been deceived by the devil or by the anti-Christ." If they were to defend themselves as expected, then the obvious question arises – Gentlemen who caused you to be born again (a miracle of GOD as you've said – but that can't be according to your logic)? If it is as you say, then the devil is the one working miracles, and you've been deceived by the devil. We don't need to listen to you! Furthermore, don't be concerned about preaching or teaching about Jesus anymore. You are a liar. YOU should stop wasting money on radio and TV broadcasts, and give the money back to the poor souls who sent you this money in the first place. You should shut down your programs and stop wasting valuable TV and radio time, as well as your breath. On the other hand, if you really are born again, and the only one performing miracles is the devil so as to lift up Jesus, then continuing with your false logic, we should conclude that we don't need to say anything to anyone because "this fallen angel is a fabulous evangelist for Christ." OOOOOPS! Again, there goes your radio ministry! Repeating what my dad would say about these things, "what a mess of rubbish!"

- Should I get rid of my earrings, my jewelry, my make-up, my perfumes, my hairstyles, etc. so as to be holy and enter into heaven or not?

GOD provides us with the story of Esther as an example of HIS blessing and provision for HIS people. The book of Esther tells us about the process that she went through, as she prepared and fixed herself to meet the king - for that moment in which GOD had already planned for her. Now, because she went through a "beautifying process" that was common for people in royalty in her day, does this mean that she was the same as the Jezebel (the queen) that so many people like to compare women to, because she also fixed herself? Was Esther a carnal, conniving, controlling, and idolatrous woman like Jezebel? No, of course not! These are two very different women in the Bible, but they both used "makeup."

This question leads me to one of my personal peeves with Christianity AND religion in general. As a religion, inherent discrimination against many things seems to be the rule. I'm not talking about the color of the skin or the rich versus the poor or Jew versus Arab or makeup versus natural or jewelry or pants or whatever. I'm talking about something far more serious – it is in fact THE HISTORICAL ISSUE OF DISCRIMINATION AGAINST WOMEN BY RELIGION and for the purpose of this commentary – the "CHRISTIAN RELIGION." This should NOT BE. In fact, in the NAME OF JESUS we – the Church of Jesus Christ - _need to get rid of discrimination and particularly the prejudice against women_ in our Christian churches! If there is a religion that SHOULD NOT DISCRIMINATE against women, it is the "Christian" religion. This sect of Judaism MUST stand firm in its defense of WOMEN. We MUST recognize that women in the Church of JESUS CHRIST are servants of GOD – it doesn't matter if they are beautiful or ugly, "dolled-up" or dressed like nuns. What they wear and how they look, should be a NON-ISSUE! If our women were to put on long white gowns when they went to church, are we going to compare them to the prostitute/priestesses of ancient Greece, where many did dress like that? No? GOD forbid? Then why is it that women going to the beauty parlor, or putting on some makeup or jewelry, causes so many men (including ministers) to have such "hissy fits of religion" comparing them to the conniving Jezebel and NOT the Godly Esther?

HELLO! Knock, Knock, anybody home? I DON'T CARE WHAT YOU THINK; when I tell you that I detest religion! In fact, AFTER I was born-again, I still didn't and don't like religion. I include here the religion of Christianity. RELIGION is not GOD. After becoming a born-again Christian (the born-again topic is covered in Lesson 2 on Water Baptism), I began to encourage and even give my wife whatever she needed, so that SHE COULD LOOK PRETTY FOR HERSELF as well as for <u>ME</u>! True she still doesn't need any of it, but that's not my point. Whenever I need to go out somewhere, I make sure my shoes are shined, my suits are impeccable, my nails properly trimmed, and that my hair is in place. Now, why is it a problem for a woman to want to do the same thing? Perhaps you may have a problem with this, but not me. If my wife wants to look her best, she should. In the same way that she doesn't object to me looking my best when I go out, I don't object to her looking her best as she goes about her day.

Since I'm on this subject, there is also the important point of why should I be excessively admiring how other ladies look, when I have a beautiful wife, and better yet she's been the wife of my youth? Men, if you were to admire how elegant or pretty she looks, there's no problem. I can handle that. Now, if you just can't take your eyes off of her and your heart starts to wander off into anything other than respectful admiration, your problem may be one of "sin at the door," as GOD warned Cain. Hello. Jesus said, *"Whosoever looks on a woman to lust after her has committed adultery with her already in his heart." Matthew 5:28*

I wonder "why is it that the Christian Religion has historically had a problem with women in leadership, and even today still has the same problem?" Is it SIN? After much thought and meditation, my conclusion is that, YES, SIN IS THE PROBLEM, BUT, it's not the women, <u>IT IS A PROBLEM WITH THE MEN</u> (including our ministers)! If we teach that something is sinful today, then it had to be sinful Ten, Twenty, 100, 500, 1000, 2000, 5000 years ago <u>ALSO</u>. If this were not the case, then our concept of an ALMIGHTY and PERFECT GOD is false. I know that the ONLY GOD I WILL SERVE is the ALMIGHTY GOD of the Bible. GOD is not a liar. Men are liars. GOD is neither going to permit something today that would then be sinful to HIM tomorrow, nor is HE going to approve of something yesterday that is going to be sinful today!

Hello Christians. Shall we act as some bands of crazed Muslims have done in their countries, beating women for wearing bras, dressing too modern, or showing their faces? Perhaps Christian women who take care to look lovely, now need to be beaten? May the LORD rebuke you!

NO. No. No! In fact, as a Puerto Rican (an ALMOST perfect macho nationality) Pastor (sorry, I forgot that I have to be humble), I assure you my great grandpas Italian DNA will want to come out just for you! If you "toucha ma wife, I breaka ju face!"

Without a doubt, we the Church need to repent of many of the same prejudices that the "world" is guilty of. My experience in the Roman Catholic Church was that Mary was "The Mother of God." Okay, I won't argue that designation, BUT my question then is "Why can't women be in ministry?" If God can choose a woman to bring and nurture HIS SON on this earth, why is it that MEN in ROME (and in many of our various denominational councils) don't want a woman as a priest or as a minister to lead us to the SON? If being a woman was to be such a problem, then why didn't the ALMIGHTY bring forth Jesus from a man? Isn't it an easy thing for the ALMIGHTY to cause a male to give birth to a child? Remember, the Bible says "but with GOD all things are possible" Matthew 19:26, BUT my point is, HE chose a woman.

After years of study of the Bible, I know that GOD IS NOT prejudiced against women. In Proverbs, WISDOM is called a "she" and THE CHURCH OF JESUS IS CALLED "THE BRIDE." In fact I could wonder, doesn't this present the problem for Christian men, of "cross dressing" or even of "gender confusion" for REAL CHRISTIAN MEN? NO, it doesn't? Good, it shouldn't!

This next point deserves its very own paragraph. IF IT IS OKAY for THE MEN of the Roman Clergy as well as other historic Christian denominations, to imagine themselves as the WIFE OF JESUS here on this earth, as they fulfill their ministerial roles, WHY CAN'T WOMEN imagine themselves as the WIFE OF JESUS and fulfill the ministerial roles of Pastors or Teachers on this earth? Humanly speaking, they are better equipped to be "wives (I'm implying as mothers and nurturers)" than the men are, and who knows, if not better equipped to be pastors and teachers than many men have been in particular instances.

What was that? Paul said what?! Hmmmm. I'll get to that in a moment but I have another rhetorical question. "Why has the Church become a man's club?" I can't understand why in the Roman Church, Mother Teresa can be beatified as a Saint, just like so many Popes and men before her were, yet while she lived she could NOT BE ALLOWED to be a priest in the same church. Did I miss a catechism class which told me that there are different classes of saints? Who would be greater in heaven – a female saint or a male? Or, are all saints equal before GOD?

Are you thinking Equal? I thought you might. Well, if GOD doesn't make any distinction among the saints, then why would we here on earth? In fact, which is greater in heaven and on earth – all the popes (the "Vicars" of Christ) put together or the woman named Mary, the one we've eloquently given the label of Mother of God? Hey, wait a minute, I need to get back to Paul; I want to remind you of what the Apostle Paul also said in Galatians 3:28 that *"...IN CHRIST there is neither male nor female."* Wow, this seems deep, AND ALSO CONTRADICTORY. Was Paul drunk? Does this make any sense, or are women equal only when it is convenient for MEN? Perhaps we need to understand that without CHRIST, men and woman want to control and dictate whatever and whomever they want. Was Paul advising young Pastor Timothy, so that any new converts from a Greek religion that held Priestesses/Prostitutes in high esteem, would realize that now they have to conform to a lifestyle of - GOD is first in - every aspect of their lives, and that self and their old religion would have to be relegated to death?

Without GOD, self always comes first. With CHRIST, men and women want to love and obey GOD. Self is now secondary and put to death. We want to please GOD. Therefore, there is a BIG difference between the children of GOD and the children of the devil. Well then, who has been in control of the "Christian religion?" Without a doubt there have been divisions and strife over the issue of women in the church, even as there was with gentiles following Jewish law. The Bible tells us that the Apostle James got up (Acts 15:13) and proposed a resolution to this Jewish/Gentile issue at that time. Why not look to his writings, so that perhaps his early wisdom can help settle this question for us today? Let's look in his epistle and see if it would help us resolve this issue. James 4:1 *"Where do wars and fights come from among you? Do they not come from your desires for pleasure that war in your members?"* Oh no! Have we been fighting and arguing because "we men" want to be in control? Worse yet, is it because we men can only see women as "desires for pleasure," and James is telling us that THAT is a work of the flesh? Oooops! Was that your toe I just stepped on?

Alright, that's enough for now. Let's move on. Sorry if you got a little confused there. It wasn't intended. I come from a family of four sisters, and I got to see some of the discrimination that they endured from the Puerto Rican "macho" culture (yes, it also existed here in the USA, just in a more subtle and educated form), when I was still a little kid, and I admit I'm still a little sensitive to this issue. Now as an adult I realize that <u>DISCRIMINATION AGAINST WOMEN IS NOT FROM GOD</u>. In fact Christians should be at the forefront of fighting for WOMENS RIGHTS! No, I'm not talking about the unbalanced and un-Christ like "Feminist" movement. I'm talking about what the Bible says in John 8:36, *"If the Son therefore shall make you free, ye shall be free indeed."* Anyway, there are so many similar questions, that we could continue endlessly discussing them.

In the examples that I have already used, I have not included some of the more useless and tempting questions that some "Christians" have asked me, such as:

•   If GOD knows everything why did he create the devil?

GOD does not create slaves. HE has created intelligent beings, capable of choosing if they are going to serve him or not. Even as he told Israel in Deuteronomy 30:19 *"I call heaven and earth as witnesses today against you, that I have set before you life and death, blessing and cursing; therefore choose life, that both you and your descendents may live."* We are the ones that don't seem to understand that GOD is not insecure of HIS Majesty and HIS power.

- If GOD knew Adam was going to eat from the tree of the knowledge of good and evil, why did HE put the tree in the garden?

Although GOD created Adam in HIS image and HIS likeness, so that Adam could be "god" in this world, GOD also wanted to establish and leave with Adam a symbol of HIS PREEMINENCE and HIS AUTHORITY, for HE is the GOD of ALL AUTHORITY and ALL POWER. Think about this. The Almighty GOD placed a symbol of HIS sovereign authority in a section of the Garden of Eden, in the form of a tree. This tree didn't interfere with Adam, it didn't threaten, and it didn't compete with Adam. So what was the problem with the tree? Actually there was none. GOD commanded man not to eat of the fruit of that tree. This seems simple enough, right? Okay, it's possible that after a long period of time, maybe after hundreds of years, you might get tired of eating the same thing all the time, year in and year out. As some children would say – "Boring!" Why not choose to try something different? Why not try the fruit from that one tree? After all, there was no such prohibition given to the animals. What could be the problem? Sounds like devils advocacy, doesn't it?

This may seem strange to you, but what is logical to me is that since the Bible does not indicate otherwise, why didn't Adam at some point; decide to get rid of this tree? After all, GOD did not tell him that he could not chop down the tree. So, what I would ask is "why didn't Adam chop down the tree?" If he had done so, it would've meant that a potential problem was removed. After all, he couldn't eat from a tree that no longer existed. Remember, the command given by GOD was that Adam should not eat of this tree. There is nowhere found any indication that he could not chop down the tree.

The Bible does not tell us specifically how long Adam was alone. Perhaps it was only a few months or perhaps it may have been thousands of years. If he was to eat of the fruit from the trees, and tend the garden, I would imagine that Adam was very busy. Possibly all the animals that he was in charge of, also had him quite entertained. Only GOD knows. Maybe I'm thinking like a New Yorker – remove the tree, end of problem! Again, if Adam had chopped down the tree, he would have avoided all the problems/prejudices that to this day we still have to deal with. Oh well.

- If GOD forgives my sins, then what's the big deal if I commit one or two more sins and then afterwards ask for his forgiveness?

1 John 1:9 says, *"If we confess our sins, he is faithful and just to forgive us our sins, and to cleanse us from all unrighteousness."* I admit that this sounds like an open invitation to keep sinning, but in Romans 6:1-6, we are informed that we cannot continue living in sin. In 1 John 3:6 we find, *"Whoever abides in Him does not sin. Whoever sins has neither seen Him nor known Him."* Actually the above question is a quasi-intellectual argument that fomented one of the early heresies to affect the primitive church (even while some of the early apostles were still living). The carnal and heretical attitude these people had, was "GOD forgives us, therefore we can sin." This became a reason for some to live in the same promiscuous and exaggerated manner that the Romans and Greeks lived in those days.

Let me move on. Of course I'm not even going to bother with some of the ridiculous "circular reasoning" type of questions I've heard since High School. For example "Can God create a rock too heavy for Him to pick up...?" If we could just step away from the endless spiral of silly questions - which do not take us to GOD, but lead us to strife, we will see that there are too many carnal things that cause us to be divided, and argue foolishly. Why is this? In my opinion, it is because of the lack of proper instruction, or the lack of listening ability (ears to hear) that too many people have. If we the teachers and pastors of today, would make effort to teach the complete counsel of GOD, and more people would earnestly pray that they would have "ears to hear what the Lord has to say," so many foolish questions would be avoided. It is my prayer before GOD, "Lord I ask that you lift up the five-fold ministry for these last days (the Apostle, Prophet, Evangelist, Pastors and Teachers), and anoint our ears to hear completely, so that we can attain the unity of faith, to the stature of the perfect man - Christ."

I can almost envision the thoughts that Paul had, in Acts 19:2, when he encountered some disciples who had not even heard of the HOLY SPIRIT! Can you imagine how the apostle Paul would react today? He would encounter not only a lack of teaching about the HOLY SPIRIT, but he would be astonished to find a church where there were no miracles, no signs and wonders, no holiness, no righteousness, and not to mention he would find an ambiguity of the gospel he knew, because of the general relativism that now seems to hold sway in our pulpits.

Here's something for you to think about today. <u>GOD did not call the apostle Paul or Peter or James or John, for this day</u>. HE CALLED AND ASSIGNED YOU AND ME to this time. Let us instruct people on how to live and preach the Word of GOD as Paul instructed in 2 Timothy 2:15 *"as a worker that needs not to be ashamed, rightly dividing the word of truth."* With the Lord's help, we can do at least as well as the Apostles did for their time, because <u>GOD chose us for this day</u> from before the foundation of the earth!

Let us make effort to reach everyone with the complete Word of GOD. We the pastors can only influence (if our influence is GOD directed) a few million people in the world, BUT that SPIRIT-LED million can be the "starter" to "turn-on" the rest of Christianity (over a billion people), who can then reach everyone else! If we – the pastors and teachers would all unite in our purpose to preach and instruct just the basics, <u>with an emphasis on personal responsibility</u> to study, meditate, teach, and live what we learn, without a doubt our churches WILL REACH the other billions around the world with the gospel of peace and life.

After so many years of participating in and observing the kingdom of GOD in action, I have come to the conclusion that there are a few things that have escaped too many of us. These few things are among the many things that do not please GOD. Our people know a number of things, but too many don't know some of the most <u>basic principles of the Bible</u>. Now don't misunderstand me. I have found Christians that are well educated by their denomination in specific areas of the Bible, and some who have a balanced and strong grounding in the Bible. Thank GOD and their teachers for this. But, I also want to caution you at the same time that too many more have also been seduced by their flesh to become "specialists or exhibitionists" in specific areas and teachings of the Bible, at the expense of other important and basic things we ALL NEED TO KNOW. As Jesus said in Matthew 23:23, "… *Pharisees, hypocrites! For ye pay tithe of mint and anise and cumin, and have omitted weightier matters of the law, judgment, mercy, and faith: these ought ye to have done, and not to leave the other undone."*

Perhaps you may not have noticed this, but we are not following the complete plan of GOD for ourselves. In Luke 4:23 Jesus quoted an existing proverb of the day *"Physician heal thyself."* I think we need to look inwards and begin the healing that needs to take place in us FIRST. What do I mean by this? Well, we generally are not the body of Christ. We aren't even Christians first. We are Baptist. We are Charismatic. We are Methodist. We are Disciples. We are Pentecostal. We are Presbyterians. We are the "this or that" church. We are "niche" specialists in the religious market. What a shame. I still remember my shock, when a dear friend told me, "I'm not Christian, I'm Roman Catholic!"

As I said, many of our churches or denominations have become "specialists" in specific areas of teaching. I don't mean to belittle the people or to imply that these churches are not churches of GOD. No. It's just that we've lost our focus as the Church of Jesus Christ, which is - TO BE LIKE JESUS. In order to continue on my premise that we have become specialists, let's look into a church that I am most familiar with. Remember, I started in the Roman Church, until my parents became born again and settled into the church that my dad's barber had suggested: the congregation that took the time to answer questions about the Bible and was located in a basement in New York, the Pentecostal Church.

Does anyone want to learn about or want to receive the baptism of the HOLY SPIRIT? Then you need to go to the place where there are real "specialists" in this area - the Pentecostal church. I personally have no doubt that over time you will receive the genuine baptism of the HOLY SPIRIT in a Pentecostal Church. Why? They actively teach and encourage people about receiving the baptism of the HOLY SPIRIT (it's difficult to receive what you've never heard about); they focus on a life of separation, a life of prayer, a life of genuinely seeking GOD, etc. The end result of living a life focused on GOD? You receive the Baptism of the HOLY SPIRIT. Isn't this interesting? Without going through a tiresome list, let's just say that there are others that have different specialties: water baptism; faith; the gifts of the Spirit; casting out demons; prophecy; holiness (no not the unfortunates that only focus on dress); worship; healing; praise, etc.

We the Church should NOT LOSE OUR FOCUS – we are TO BE LIKE JESUS CHRIST. That is the only properly balanced and complete counsel of GOD. Why? Every church should reflect the biblical and universal church - the body of Christ here on this earth (no, I'm not speaking about the Roman Catholic Church, which falsely claims to be the "only" legitimate church forgetting even the Orthodox congregations).

Other than the one time Jesus commanded HIS followers "not to leave Jerusalem, but to wait for the promise." At no other time did Jesus instruct the church to go to a particular area or to a particular house so that they could receive a special teaching or hidden truth or another promise, which was not readily available to everyone else. Shouldn't we and our congregations speak everything that the Bible tells us GOD has offered to the world?

Some people have also defended the particular focus of their denomination by saying, "Pastor, we have to teach people that drinking wine is sin." Or "We have to teach that women wearing pants is sinful." Or, "We have to teach that women should cover their head." Or, "Pastor, you know that if we're not baptized immediately, we won't be saved." And so on. Well, GOD has not authorized us to add or take away from what HE has already said. "But Pastor, that's what the Bible says!"

Family, the Bible says many things that we have conveniently ignored. Perhaps you should review the question I covered, regarding *"Should I get rid of my earrings, my jewelry, my make-up, my perfumes, my hairstyles, etc., so as to be holy and enter into heaven or not?"* Maybe you should also meditate on my musings on "Why is the Church still a man's club?" Hopefully you will get stirred up! We tend to look at some things so narrowly, that we forget that "GODS thoughts are so much higher than our thoughts." If we seek GOD and focus on what HE wants, we will reflect JESUS CHRIST! Now, THAT is what GOD WANTS! There will be no more wars, dissensions, arguments, etc., amongst us. Instead we will see things from GOD'S viewpoint. In the case of women, we will defend the GOD GIVEN RIGHTS of our Christian moms, sisters, daughters, nieces, and granddaughters, to freely MOVE and WORK in this world and in the KINGDOM OF GOD and HIS RIGHTEOUSNESS! People, GOD has given us His Complete Counsel – the Bible. Let's know it.

I'm going to obey GOD, and not man. What is written is written. For example: why would Jesus turn water into something that would be "sinful" to the people of the wedding party he was attending? Oh? It wasn't real wine? It was unfermented grape juice? He was just a great illusionist? Okay, then why is it that Noah drank wine (unfermented grape juice?) and got drunk (this was the man spared by GODS grace) to the point that he fell asleep naked in his tent? I have yet to find somewhere in the Bible that indicates that he was condemned for this. Or why would GOD command Jeremiah to go to the house of the Rechabites to bring them to the house of the Lord, and give them wine (again not unfermented grape juice) to drink? Was GOD going against HIS own commands? Or how about the woman brought to Jesus for she was found in the act of adultery, and yet she was let go with the command "Go and sin no more." Wait. Why was David labeled as a man "after GODS own heart" when he was a murderer, a liar, and an adulterer? King Saul seemed to be a much more righteous and moral man by comparison. This is not to justify wanton living, or focus on newer biblical interpretation of custom. It is to make the point that GOD will not tempt man to sin; instead HE focuses on the godliness of self restraint and obedience, and above all on HIS MERCY. Okay, let's not get too deep into these things now. From time to time we focus on some of these things at LA ROCA Church, but perhaps, at some point I'll start up a website or a "blog" where we can discuss these things in a little more depth, while giving greater access to the people of other congregations.

GOD'S interest in man (by the way this means our species) is to SAVE MANKIND completely. Can we make that our interest also? Let's teach EVERYONE, that what we need to emphasize and teach is: <u>we must reflect Christ in everything</u>.

It is such a shame to see so many people trying to build magnificent projects for the Glory of GOD, upon incomplete foundations. Without a doubt, when we do this, we are inviting the wholesale destruction of these projects, with the accompanying personal distress, family stress, and perhaps even the despair of the churches that we attend. Over the years, my heart has cried and suffered with my brothers in Christ, as I have seen their work and their ministries collapse and break apart, when the waves and the winds of torment came upon their lives.

GOD has designed us to be perfect instruments. HE has designed a process for us that will cause us to shine and excel! If we would only learn to establish our foundation firmly upon the Word, we would avoid the pain caused by the loss of things that we knew were not approved by the Lord Himself (remember it is His Kingdom). What I mean by this, is that when we are busy in the Kingdom of GOD, we sometimes make decisions that although they seem logical at the time - we forgot to ask GOD'S permission before we made those decisions. At other times we think that the busier we are the more pleasing we are to GOD, even when we know that we may make poor choices because of the constant juggling that we're doing, since after all, "we are doing so much for GOD!"

Now I don't mean to say that we are unable to make our own decisions, so that when the storms do come, everything will turn out okay. No. What I mean is that we run the risk of following our intellect, when we make decisions, but it was not GOD'S perfect plan or time for us. Putting it another way, we chose what GOD did not want for us at that moment in time. This can happen even in those things that for us seem so simple, but nevertheless GOD still wants us to ask him anyway. In my life, my desire to separate myself from useless religion sometimes did cause me to make some poor choices. For example I know that in religion, in order to NOT make a decision we religiously say "let's pray about it." Since there were times when I should have prayed about some "simple" things first, my desire to NOT be religious caused me not to pray first. The point I'm making is, that unless it is something that is clearly written about in the Bible, we need to seek the counsel and direction of GOD for everything. Remember, HE is GOD. Everything HE does is perfect.

Sometimes, at the moment that we make our decisions, we may feel a tinge of uncertainty in our spirit and we resort to another religious attitude: I'm making those decisions "by faith." The result is that when the time of testing arrives, what has not been approved by GOD is typically taken by the wind, burned by the fire, or shaken to the ground.

This shouldn't be. I'm not talking about the winds and the waves that GOD informed us would come. No, these will always come. Instead I'm talking about the imperfect decisions that cause our work to be ill prepared to resist the winds and the waves that come. As members of the body of Christ, we should not be ignorant or allow ourselves to be poorly taught in the full counsel of GOD. Please know this; I'm not talking about intellectual, decision making exercises! I'm talking about a life that follows and imitates Jesus!

Why is it that so many Christians, some with many years of experience, still demonstrate a tendency towards error or incredulity – especially when we are dealing with the basic and beginning principles of the Bible? Why do so many still run after what seems new, or cool in the gospel? Why do pastors continue to run after too many sheep, so as to again and again teach them about the most basic and foundational truths of the Bible? How easily too many people are deceived! Sometimes I wonder if we truly are the pastors of goats or donkeys, rather than sheep.

After facing these issues in various churches over the years, as a teacher and as a pastor, I have come to the conclusion that solid foundational principles of the Bible have not been set in most believers lives. On the contrary, what I have seen are churches, denominations, councils, ministers, and individuals that are busily running at breakneck speeds, to establish their own kingdoms, and their own dominions, lifting up their own egos, instead of the genuine Kingdom of our Lord Jesus Christ.

Thank GOD that there are still many pastors and ministers that have no interest in profiting from their own fame or personal adulation, instead their interest is still serving the Great and Almighty GOD through HIS Son Jesus. Unfortunately, we the Pastors too often don't have the time or the prepared assistants for the labor we have before us. If we did, perhaps we could take the time to carefully examine the foundations of each member that we have or that come and join our flock (I think most of us have also gotten a few of the many pretty butterflies that are just passing through).

It is with good helpers that we can examine and research where there are weak areas in the foundations of the people we receive. It is how we can determine where there needs to be repairs or where strengthening needs to occur, in order to overcome the sloppy or incomplete workmanship in the foundations of our people. If we only knew every persons background, and what they needed (and these people were interested in submitting to the teachings of the Bible), we could immediately begin to repair and rebuild these foundations with the PERFECT and DIVINE materials that have been given to us by GOD.

Pastors, teachers, don't feel disheartened or incapable. People can be flaky, and vicious, but remember, GOD is on our side. The Bible says in Philippians 1:6, *"Being confident of this very thing, that HE which hath begun a good work in you will perform it until the day of Jesus Christ."* I believe that GOD will lift up His Glorious Church. Without a doubt, we need the help of the HOLY SPIRIT, as never before, but we know HE'S with us; guiding, strengthening, and helping us to finish HIS Perfect work – CHRIST IN US.

The outlines that follow this introductory discourse began to form during the founding and establishment of the first church planting in New York City in 1984. It is with deep stirrings in my heart, that I remember how GOD began to move in such a wonderful way with the inexperienced and untried pastor that I was in 1984. The congregation began to arise and multiply in a powerful way. In five Sundays, just by word of mouth, we had more than 55 people with us! We ended up renting meeting rooms at the Holiday Inn in mid-Manhattan, so as to accommodate the people. How did this happen to me? I had no fame, I wasn't a singing sensation, or a famous musician, or famous ex-criminal, or a great orator, or even an established minister. I was just a young man determined to be obedient to the call of GOD, to "go and preach" in New York City.

As I now understand, in the middle of any move of GOD, GOD allows the devil to shake the work, so as to remove what is not fruitful or healthy. As I said before, the moment arrives when the winds and the waves begin to assault our lives. The church in New York divided. A few individuals without solid foundations in the Word, jealous and carnal (since they were not being led by the Spirit of GOD), full of envy (as the Bible says "Where do Wars and dissensions come from?), arose against me and the work that had begun. Although these individuals had previously been members of other churches for a number of years, they demonstrated their immaturity and unfaithfulness in the Kingdom, and in the Bible, by allowing their carnal and selfish desires to be instruments of wind, rain, and waves, to attack our new congregation. Was it GOD? No. GOD allowed it, but it was the devil and his human instruments. I thank GOD that He turned this treachery into opportunities for continued growth in my wife and I.

When from one day to another, a church begins to undergo division, we need to examine James chapter four. The purpose of these divisions is to destroy and weaken - not so much the congregation, as it is geared to destroy and weaken the pastor. As the Bible says, "Smite the Shepherd, and the sheep will be scattered" (Zechariah 13:7) If it is possible, the individuals at the heart of these divisions are seeking to replace the Pastor, with someone that is more to their liking. They always want someone that thinks as they do, and that will do as they say and NOT what GOD says. Now my question is, "Does this sound like the move of the Spirit of GOD?" Absolutely not! It doesn't matter if they couch their words with quotes from the Bible, so as to justify their decisions. If you carefully examine what they are quoting, you will inevitably find that they are incorrectly applying the Word of GOD to situations that don't exist or that they've invented! It is envy, anger, enmity, dissension, etc. that has motivated too many, to perpetuate such treachery across the ages (Galatians 5:17-21). The Bible teaches us that these things are the works of the flesh, since the precious fruits of the Spirit are: love, kindness, goodness, gentleness, etc. (Galatians 5:22, 23). In fact I have found no evidence <u>that a church was ever divided</u> by these fruits!

After more than 24 years of ministry, my wife and I have witnessed these things happening too frequently in the Kingdom of GOD. We all agree that it is the Spirit of GOD that adds to the church those that are to be saved. But, who then divides and takes people out from the churches? After all, these are the people that the Bible says were added by the HOLY SPIRIT. Is it GOD that inspires the individuals busily working at destroying or dividing the churches (as I said, trying to destroy the pastors NOT the congregation)? No! It is the devil manipulating the tools that we continually lug around and provide - the desires of the flesh.

When we ALL understand that divisions, dissensions, and wars proceed from our own carnal desires, we will resist these desires until they no longer control us! When we really truly learn to do this, the number of little churches in our cities will begin to diminish. Cities won't BE SO FULL of tiny churches on every corner! Many of which are by-products of divisions of other congregations. Well, should I say it? Yes I must. ***Our cities are full of small churches that are ineffective, inefficient, intolerant, and without divine purpose or natural and spiritual influence.*** (Of course I don't mean to say that all small churches are ineffective or inefficient. No. Having been raised in a small church that never grew big, I know that they sent out dozens of pastors, teachers, missionaries, etc. to the field.) On the other hand, if we are truly the church of Christ, we'd be ready and powerful in contesting every work and inch that the devil desires to wrest from us!

Let's look at how our Jewish brethren operate. Their synagogues aren't on every corner. They're NOT looking to establish their rabbi's Kingdom. They're not one another's competition or enemy. On the contrary, they unite immediately to face off against any enemy that arises against any of them. They are family. They are friends. In fact, they are the living breathing history of GOD at work with humanity. The way Jews operate, is exactly how the "primitive" or early Christian church operated.

It is time the Church of Jesus Christ had completed the spread of the Gospel throughout the known world! The technology, the means of travel and the education levels for the spread of the Gospel have been here for multiple decades now. But what has happened? The enemy has disguised himself, so that he is even in our own midst! In these days we are fighting against a satanic wave of idolatry and false gods in the church that is incredible. You may ask, "How is this pastor?" Well it's not something new or fancy that is passing by. It's the same old god. Hidden and false, that proceeds from the devil himself. This god is called the "Id" or "me" or "mine" or "Self." This sin of prideful SELF worship and idolatry (I want, need, and deserve…) is destroying many people in our churches, and running rampant throughout our society.

"How is that possible, pastor? You're talking about the church of Jesus." No, I'm not talking about the genuine church. I'm talking about individuals that actually "play" church, and are in love with "self" and have no room for GOD or anyone else in their lives. The commandment is, "You shall have no other GOD," but they don't know how or why they need to fight against their own "self interest." In fact we are so focused on self that we forget that there is an ALMIGHTY GOD who watches us and waits for us to turn our thoughts and plans to HIM. Can you imagine that the ALMIGHTY is as interested as we are about our protruding chins, or the overly large or misshaped noses that we're going to have to have surgery on, or the other things that we give so much importance to? Unfortunately, while we focus on self, there is no interest in learning or applying the truths of the Bible. No.

I've heard that as we grow older we get wiser. This is possibly true, since so many people typically don't have any interest in GOD until they get much older (or at least until they get over the idea that they're invincible and are going to last almost forever). Unfortunately, it may be when they're older that they'll begin to consider that what the Bible says may be true, when they hear or read "that the beginning of wisdom is the fear of the Lord." It really is too bad that most of us put eternity as something that's very far off, and focus too much on the split second of time called "life." As I've left the years of brash youthfulness behind, I've come to understand that people want to hear what they want to hear, and they're going to do what they want to do.

In at least the last twenty-five years, we've been bombarded with self-centered messages. I remember as a little kid, when President Kennedy said, "Ask not what your country can do for you, but ask what you can do for your country." After Madison Avenue began their message "that you deserve the very best," it seemed to pick up speed, until we now live in a society that is producing people who can only think about "self." There's now widespread selfishness across America, as it is in the rest of the world, where almost everything is focused on "what's in it for me." If look momentarily at our political system, we find our politicians are like that. It's not "I'm here to serve my country," no. In fact we see them typically following their own agenda once in office, without much regard for the people who elected them. Why? They've found other entrenched and powerful members who've enticed them with the drug of power and influence. Once newly elected politicians are hooked, they also get "high" with these senior "influence peddlers." They've discovered a drug they can legally use, making easy money at the expense of others.

Probably one of the scariest times for most politicians is Election Day. If people would only realize that most of the people they've elected to office, paying them a regular salary, will complete their elected terms as millionaires, it would perhaps cause us to push for term limits. Okay,

I said a momentary look at politics. Rather than get angry, we need to laugh at what WE THE PEOPLE have done. We Americans deserve the very best? Well, you got it. Self-interest is why politicians can get away with taking credit for "inventing the internet," informing us "they didn't know" or "they didn't realize they broke the law" (oh by the way, most of them are lawyers!), and so on! Yes they've taken to heart the Madison Avenue message that "they <u>deserve</u> what they now have." They deserve to be coddled and pampered.

Although I don't want to equate Madison Avenue to the devil, we Christians have swallowed their marketing campaign, and aligned ourselves with the same idea that caused Lucifer to be cast out from heaven. We want to be told that we should be rich and powerful, and that this is a gift of GOD to us! We deserve this. I remember as a kid, hearing the story of "Pedro." It goes something like this: *We're a little bored and want someone to play with, even though we were told by our mom to stay put take care of our little sibling and behave. MOM! Pedro's bothering me! MOM!? (Then conspiratorially we tell our little brother, come on Pedro bother me, come-on do it again – because we liked it.)* Are we trying to do the same thing to GOD? We know HIS commandments, but maybe they're boring us. *LORD! The devil is bothering me! LORD?! Do something. Then almost conspiratorially we check what we know is "ungodly," come on devil, send me more stuff - after all it just came in our email. LORD?! The devil is really bothering me!* What we forget is that GOD knows our hearts. HE knows that we want the devil to do it again, for we really don't mind. After all, why can't we have a little excitement? Come on, somebody tell me how good I am, how I deserve this. We'll even ask the LORD, "how come YOU don't speak to me?" Come on LORD send someone to "encourage me." Of course when we do trip over ourselves, like politicians we say, "I didn't know." Or "I thought it was you LORD" or if cornered, we'll even admit, "I did wrong, forgive me." After all, what is GOD going to do, throw us away? NAAAH. That'll never happen.

For too many of us, our god has become self. The personal "I am" is now god. Perhaps we're not playing with the devil; it's just that we don't realize that the devil is playing with us. After all, we're in the Kingdom of GOD. "I know am a teacher." "I know I am more intellectual than most." "Hey, I went to Harvard or Yale or Cornell and am better prepared." "I speak in tongues and am led by the Spirit of GOD." "I am the anointed." "I am more compassionate than others." "I have a better vocabulary; therefore I am a better speaker." "I have a better voice." "I know what the church needs." "I founded this church." "I know that without me, the pastor could do nothing." "Whenever I come in, GOD manifests Himself." And so on. This false god of self, with its false prophets has been manifesting itself in and through our councils, the churches, assemblies, sects, and individuals throughout this land, because there is no correct teaching of the full counsel of GOD to counteract these surreptitious lies. Where are the men and women of GOD, who are full of: Humbleness, Holiness, Love, Peace, Good Works, Hope, Meekness, Joy, Faith, Obedience to the Word, etc.?

If you happen to be one of those that have been deceived to serve this false god, of self-love and pride - REPENT! TURN AROUND and TURN TO GOD. HE doesn't want you to perish. HE will have mercy upon you, BUT RUN TO HIM NOW! Separate yourself from the path you have been walking and the things that you're doing! Ask for forgiveness from GOD. Go to your pastor and teachers and ask for their forgiveness, especially if you know you've offended them. Finally, go to all the brethren that you were about to hurt because of your idolatry towards self and ask for their forgiveness! In fact, ask your pastor if it would be wise for you to stay at your local congregation or if they recommend that you go somewhere else for awhile, in order to receive healing and restoration. It's possible you may actually need to take a short sabbatical, so as not to be a disturbance to anyone. As servants of GOD they will send you where you can be restored without affecting others at your church. Then, when you are healed and restored, you can return and be the helper that GOD wants you to be to your pastor and to the congregation that HE placed you in.

LORD, WE NEED YOUR HELP! Have mercy upon us, and heal us of this "self-loving and deceptive" disease of pride and self. We do not deserve anything, except to repent and throw ourselves at YOUR MERCY. Deliver us from such a contagious and malignant lie! Family of GOD, right now I hear the Spirit of GOD telling me, "It is time to mature and walk towards the unity of faith and the stature of <u>The Perfect Man</u> – JESUS CHRIST."

It was after much prayer and personal anguish that I realized that the first storm that I went through in ministry helped and strengthened me. I also began to understand the lack of basic teaching that was missing in the lives of the people at our church. I asked the Lord to grant me that, from that point until my work was finished in the City, the numerical growth of our congregation would be slow and gradual. I wanted them to have time to grow and mature.

How strange my prayer had become! I was actually wondering if I was going against some sort of biblical principle, since I now wasn't in a rush to get people into our congregation, so as to prove the call of GOD upon my life. Now I only wanted people saved, and delivered but I was in no rush for them to settle into our congregation. Without knowing it, the Lord was teaching me and leading my prayer. It is THE LORD who places people into our congregations. It is not what you or I want. As you go through "Lesson A1" in the Appendix section, you will understand more about this.

When I would say to the Lord in my prayers, that I wanted to build and establish a good foundation in people regarding the central truths of the Bible (so that the people that I taught would not so easily be shaken in whatever other storms may pass by them), I was actually saying that <u>I wanted to disciple people</u>. The vision of planting a local church, that the Lord had given me, was now extending itself more and more. The vision of a well taught local church was expanding. Now I saw that the local church should be a beautiful microcosm of the overall Kingdom of GOD, moving forward and producing disciples everywhere we went. My focus had now become - prepare leaders, wherever I went, ready for the work of the harvest for the last days of the Church of Christ. I now knew that the work of the ministry didn't start and end with me. This was a team effort. It was the HOLY SPIRIT guiding me, as I taught and encouraged others, so that they could teach and encourage additional people, and on and on. I realize that everyone didn't understand, but many did.

To this day, I am grateful that The Lord granted me the opportunity to "lend" some people from our congregation in New York, to other ministries so that the work of the gospel would continue unfaltering and victorious. From time to time, I have the privilege of godly people thanking me for things such as: "I thank you pastor for the honor and confidence that you placed in me, to pastor for a year at such and such a place." A good example of this is when I go visit the island of Puerto Rico. I feel humbled before God, when I visit my Sunday school teacher from when I was a kid. I had the honor of being the pastor of this great teacher when he became a member of the church I was pastor of. This elderly man thanks me almost every time I visit, for the trust and confidence that I placed in him when I had him pastor a church in Brooklyn NY for a year. What a privilege to be in The Kingdom of GOD.

Although I was excited and motivated to plant a church in NYC back in 1984, after the "wind, the rain, and the shaking storm went by," I knew that I had work to do. I started to write, study, and organize a series of lesson outlines at the beginning of the New Year (1985). Initially these lessons comprised a series of 12 study outlines, but which now (after going through a few more storms), consist of a minimum of 28 lessons that everyone in our congregation has to go through. Without a doubt, this attitude of teaching and training has been of great encouragement to my wife and me, as well as to the people of the congregations that we've been able to minister to in these last few years.

Although we now know more of the plan of GOD for our lives, my wife and I, from time to time continue to pass through "the fire." We now understand and teach, that this is never meant to hurt or destroy us, but to reveal GOD in us! It is true that these processes are never pleasant when they first begin. In fact, too often we see these "trials" as outright and vicious attacks of the enemy, but again, my wife and I have come to understand that GOD uses circumstances, problems, and even the devil, to refine us and perfect us for His Glory. "Almighty GOD, I thank you Lord for the work that you have continued to perform and perfect in us. Manifest your Glory, for you are worthy of the best that is in us."

It's not unusual for me to remind our congregation of what the Apostle Paul told his young protégé - pastor Timothy in his second letter, 2 Timothy 2:15 *"Study to show yourself approved unto GOD, a workman that needs not to be ashamed, rightly dividing the word of truth."* Now let me pause a moment. Although I'm promoting how important it is to study and know the Bible, I have to emphasize that **this cannot be done effectively, without the direction and instruction of the HOLY SPIRIT.** If we try to study the Bible without the help of the HOLY SPIRIT, we are going to waste much precious time. How is this? Unfortunately our flesh will get in the way, and we may become hardened towards the voice of GOD, because we will begin to get puffed up (full of ourselves). Now, please understand that if we've been called to any of the "fivefold" ministry (Apostle, Prophet, Evangelist, Pastor and Teacher), GOD will break us apart, humble us and re-form us so that HE can use us. Sooner or later (pray that it is sooner) GOD will deal with our pride as HE begins to light our way with HIS precious Truth. I'm speaking from experience. We can memorize the Bible and remember loads of Bible data, but this will not make us wiser, only proud of our effort and ability.

We need to know that only GOD is our source of wisdom. The Bible tells us clearly in Proverbs 9:10 that *"the fear of the Lord is the beginning of Wisdom."* The Bible also instructs us in James 1:5, *"if any of you lacks wisdom, let him ask of GOD, who gives to all liberally and without reproach, and it will be given to him. But let him ask in faith, with no doubting, for he who doubts is like a wave of the sea driven and tossed by the wind."* The Bible also tells us in Romans 8:14, "for as many as are led by the Spirit of God, these are the sons of GOD." Notice it doesn't say "led by their intellect."

Here are a couple of things I've learned that may be helpful to you: First, your flesh is NOT what leads you to the truth of GOD. On the other hand, your flesh will lead you to almost everything that sets itself in opposition to GOD. Second, your mind (intellect) or heart (emotions) will not lead you to the truth of GOD. Only the HOLY SPIRIT can lead us to the truth of GOD. It is the HOLY SPIRIT that can teach us what GOD wants.

The HOLY SPIRIT is the only One who knows the mysteries of the Father. HE is the one that will tell us what we need to say. HE is GOD. Our earthly mind, although marvelous, cannot comprehend spiritual things. GOD is so much more than we can even imagine.

Now, please don't misunderstand when I write **"this cannot be done effectively, without the direction and instruction of the HOLY SPIRIT."** I'm not talking about discarding your intellect and I'm not talking about the baptism of the HOLY SPIRIT (although these are important), nor am I talking about the instruction of your pastors or teachers led by the Spirit of GOD (although this is important), or any of the other things that may quickly come to our minds. The direction and instruction of the Spirit that I am emphasizing, goes far beyond seminary (even though this is important), it goes far beyond the "mystical, divine revelation" that many promote (and this may be important). What GOD wants, is that you know the Author of The Word, and only the HOLY SPIRIT can lead you to HIM who is the author. THIS IS WHAT IS IMPORTANT TO GOD.

I HAVE NO DOUBT THAT GOD can use any of the aforementioned ways to impact us by His HOLY SPIRIT. After all, we know that when HE wants to get our attention, HE will! We can read how HE even used a mule to get the undivided attention of the prophet Balaam as found in Numbers 22:23 (I wonder, did the mule go to a special school to learn the language?). How about you? What is needed to get your attention? I've heard testimonies of sickness, disease, loss, etc., being used by GOD to get some peoples attention. I hope that this book will be used by GOD to get your attention and help you get aligned with what GOD wants in your life. I'm personally not interested in hearing a testimony about how your cat or dog had to have a serious talk with you!

There is a personal work of the HOLY SPIRIT that has to take place **IN US**, so that we can decide to seek GOD and only HIM. This can only happen when you humble yourself and present yourself continually before GOD with sincere prayer, to ask HIM to give you wisdom and understanding of HIS Word. This is the continual work of the HOLY SPIRIT. HE will lead you to Christ, so that you can get to know HIM, and then through CHRIST, HE will lead you to ALMIGHTY GOD, so that you can also get to know HIM. Right now, make the decision that you are going to seek HIM, with all of your strength, with all of your mind, with all of your heart! If you do this, the Bible says that YOU WILL FIND HIM!

Why don't you ask the Lord to show you what exactly you need to do to please HIM and draw you closer to HIM? I'm writing about you - closeting yourself with the Lord, so as to develop that pure, intimate, and revealing relationship with GOD that you truly desire. It is this intimate relationship that GOD wants from us. It is this type of loving relationship that will cause us to arise as "a voice calling in the desert, to prepare the way for the LORD." It is this type of unique relationship that will cause us to become the mouthpiece of GOD. It is this type of pure relationship that will cause us to become TRUE AMBASSADORS for Christ.

Now, dear reader, I want to inform you that IT IS THE SPIRIT OF GOD that will take you through the "Valley of the shadow of death." HE will take you where the "winds blow," but not so that you should perish or become disheartened. NO! The Spirit of GOD will lead you to where you will learn to depend upon HIM and not be fearful, because HE is with you, and you will learn to receive comfort from HIS rod and HIS staff as HE Shepherds you (Psalms 23:4). GOD is the GOD of order. HE wants you to be in HIS order. HE wants you to stop living in your own wisdom, in your own strength, in your own ability, so that you can step up to HIS dimension, by learning to trust completely in HIM.

It is GOD'S plan and purpose for you to stop living as the unfaithful, unjust, unwise, and unloving world continues to do. It is GODS plan that you allow Christ to arise in you and live in you. Then you will arise with the wisdom of the "Author and finisher of our faith" – Jesus Christ.

Are you ready right now? GOD is ready to help you reach those heavenly levels that HE has prepared for you. GOD is ready to give you revelation of HIS WORD. GOD is ready to teach you how to live a life that is pleasing to HIM. HE is ready to guide your steps so that you totally REFLECT JESUS.

As our dearly loved Pastor Jason Alvarez of Love of Jesus Family Church would say – "Get Ready, Get Ready, Get Ready!"

"Lord, in the Name of Jesus, let all the words that are written here, touch the hearts and souls of every reader, for eternity, and let these comments and outlines impact every reader for the rest of their earthly lives, as YOU perfect the work that YOU have begun in each of them."

Since my college years, where I studied Architecture, I began to work in the technical and industrial world for more than 30 years now. Since the time I first began working at the architectural firm of Liebman Liebman & Associates in New York City (part-time while still at college), I began to learn and understand the importance of checking the designs and jobs that we did, in every manner possible. It wasn't just the math and the aesthetics that I learned in college, but it now also included a detailed review of the financial cost for the benefit of the clients. The Liebmans and the other architects in that office, taught me to critique every phase of design as if I were an adversary (even if it was my very own favorite design!). I was now my own worse enemy looking to exploit whatever weakness or fault that I could find. It was as if every bit of work that I did was now a dissertation that had to be defended from every vicious attack. I cannot express my thanks to the late Liebman brothers for their transference of outright excellence in their work as well as the concern for their clients, in everything that they did. These were such valuable and important lessons for me, especially when a few years later I was given the opportunity to design biotech research equipment for a great family owned, billion dollar scientific company. When I got there, I had already learned that every project had to be severely tested, viciously judged, examined, and approved before it went out the door.

For the purposes of this book, I will call this process I encountered at work, and which I have seen first hand in the work of GOD in my life and that of so many others, as the **PROCESS OF EVALUATION AND APPROVAL** (which I will shorten to the acronym the **"PEA")**. Now, at the time that I was at Liebman & Associates, I did not understand that this was the divine principle expressed in *1 Peter 1:7* " *That the genuineness of your faith, being much more precious than gold that perishes, though it is tested by fire, may be found to praise, honor, and glory at the revelation of Jesus Christ."*

In the biotech industry, the PEA principle was reinforced almost fanatically. Even if a product might be able to save a persons life, it was not allowed to go out the door and get to market without first passing through the PEA. And, that was for ALL the stages of design, evaluation, and testing – in other words - at every step of the design, development, and manufacturing of the product. Considering that the company was in business to make money, even before getting a single penny of profit from any product, that product had to pass the PEA. It didn't matter if there was a long delay before we could begin to profit from it (well it did matter to the owners, but we could not let our desire or their desire for profit intervene with the safety and effectiveness of that product). It was imperative that every stage of the products design and manufacture was evaluated, tested, and approved. The danger in not diligently and completely evaluating every segment of the product was that someone could die or be severely injured (not to mention the massive lawsuits that could occur).

With the possible exception of the EXTREMELY RARE miracles that GOD in HIS infinite wisdom grants us, everything has to go through the PEA, along with the accompanying lapse of time. The initial design for everything, we understand from the Bible, occurred at the creation of the universe. GOD alone is perfect and HIS designs are perfect! BUT we, on the other hand, need help.

I want to confirm by the Bible that the PEA principle was established by GOD. Without deviating too much from the laws that GOD has established for us to have success in everything, I want to direct your attention to four biblical sections (utilizing what the Scriptures sets as the Law of Witnesses to establish a Biblical truth), where we will see that GOD wants us to be completely prepared for His work. Once again – ARE YOU READY? This principle affects your soul, body, and spirit. Are you ready for the process that GOD has prepared for you? Wooooo Hooooo! REJOICE! GOD has some "fabulous" tests (trials) for you!

- First Witness: James 1:2-4 says *"My brethren, count it all joy when you fall into various trials, knowing that the testing of your faith produces patience. But let patience have its perfect work, that you may be perfect and complete, lacking nothing."*

These verses in James let us know that there is a process of time that has to take place in order to produce patience. "The testing" is a process that produces patience. It doesn't say or imply that after enduring a small headache you will have the "patience of Job." Neither does it say that after resisting the first temptation, you're going to walk on water. No. There is a process of time that you have to go through. You will "fall into various trials." It doesn't specify what the time period is. It just implies that there is a period of time. The word "various" implies different kinds, a variety or diversity, stages or steps or numerous. It implies a passage of time. The verse indicates that after the testing of your faith, NOT during, NOT BEFORE. This patience will have its perfect work. This is the divine principle of the "PEA." GOD is in no rush. (I know. Don't you just hate it?)

GOD is the embodiment of PERFECT PATIENCE. GOD knows that the design is perfect; He only requires the process of time and evaluation to add the finishing touches to COMPLETE the work. He will continue evaluating you, until He is satisfied. Ooooops! There's a slight smudge just behind the third hair on the right of your left eyebrow. I know, no one could have noticed it, BUT GOD DID! When HE finishes with you, your faith is always going to walk around accompanied by patience. You will NO LONGER be STRESSED. You will no longer be ANXIOUS. You will no longer be AFRAID. You will no longer wonder "Is GOD GOING TO DO IT?" You will be completely at peace, completely satisfied, reflecting everything that is the LORD.

GOD knows the PEA that is perfect for you. Now, I want to assure you that it's not going to be a test or a TRIAL of one or two days, in order for you to look just like Jesus. No! I'm very sure (although I may not know you personally) that you're GOING TO NEED A NUMBER OF DIFFERENT TRIALS, even if it's just so that you will have a little bit more faith in GOD. HE knows exactly what "screws or bolts" need to be tightened in your life so that you will learn to trust HIM completely. GOD also knows what areas in your life need to be "sanded or ground down and polished." Perhaps your temper requires a little bit of adjustment. Don't worry. GOD knows exactly what to do. HE probably has prepared "Sister Coarse" to love you (you know her as Deaconess Coarse Sandpaper) – oooops! Sorry if that's your wife! No insult was intended. GOD has prepared what you need. Wait. Maybe you need some serious time of fellowship with the File family (Brother Cutting is a real favorite of The Lord) in order to bring out the Love of Jesus in you. GOD knows exactly what tools to use, and HE has them ready and waiting for you!

GOD knows exactly what needs to be tested, in order to establish the limits and the shine that He has assigned for you. HE is determined that you will be magnificent and perfect! HE has the perfect PEA waiting for you. Know this - HE will feed you PEA'S until you finally get to the point where YOU ARE COMPLETE! Come on. Eat your vegetables! As my oldest sister says "deeeto ("ay bendito" is a Puerto Rican expression for - you poor thing). She just condenses it further)!"

Get Ready, Get Ready, Get Ready! Here come the winds and the waves! Can you imagine how many things there are that GOD still has to perfect in your life? ALL THOSE THINGS and more, need to undergo the PEA. My brethren, this process will not end until you reach the level of completion (perfection) that GOD wants from you. Now, wait – there's more. WHAT!? That was ONLY the FIRST WITNESS!

- <u>Second Witness</u>: 1 Thessalonians 5:23 says, *"Now may the GOD of peace Himself sanctify you completely; and may your whole spirit, soul, and body be preserved blameless at the coming of our Lord Jesus Christ."*

This verse in Thessalonians also tells us that there is a process of time. "The GOD of peace Himself" will SANCTIFY you (separate you, as in separating the wheat from the chaff) COMPLETELY. What a privilege. GOD HIMSELF has taken us on, as HIS project! That means you will be sifted, examined, and sifted again. You will be polished, cleaned, and polished again! You will be melted, and re-melted again! Understand this - the word "completely" includes our passing thoughts, and even those we haven't had yet! Our spirit, soul, and body have to be blameless, for that great moment of the return of our LORD. Completely – without fault (or omissions), without errors, without forgetting anything. **We will be the perfect and complete product that GOD designed.** GET READY!

- <u>Third Witness</u>: 3 John 2 *"Beloved, I pray that you may prosper in all things and be in health, just as your soul prospers."*

This verse also let's us understand that there is a process of time ("that you may" – affects the present and future as also "be in health" – which also affects the present and future), since the SPIRIT of GOD desires for us to PROSPER IN EVERYTHING (the verse is for the present and the future). Now, to reach all that, there has to be a PEA. You cannot be prospered (completed) until you can demonstrate HIS approval. This is the PEA that GOD has for you. Better yet, the SPIRIT is including your health (I see this as to be in health in all things – yep, you guessed it, you need to kick those old habits!) not for a short period of time - but FOR LIFE.

- <u>Fourth Witness (I'm including this just in case you still had doubts)</u>: Ecclesiastes 3: 1 *"To everything there is a Season, a time for every purpose under heaven."*

One more time, <u>in the perfect work that GOD does in us, there is a process of time that takes place during the PEA period.</u> We all understand that we pass through periods of time as humans. We were "newborn." Then as time passed, we reached the age of "toddler." Eventually, we reached the age of "teenager" and then "adulthood," which in the process of GOD is that period of time when the perfect man – Jesus is manifested in us. As I teach our congregation – everything means EVERYTHING (it even includes the "nada" what doesn't exist)!! Every atom, nucleus, electron, proton, boson, etc., that makes you who you are, has to be checked by GOD!

The Bible helps us to understand a little bit of how magnificent is our GOD. HE is Omniscient. HE alone is perfect. HE doesn't commit errors, nor is HE lacking in intelligence. The Creator of the universe is the GOD of plans and purposes. Although we may give up and think that we can't do it, HE already has formulated HIS plan for us and <u>HE NEVER FAILS</u>. HIS divine process is infallible. HIS process in our lives, even though it takes time (and this is the process HE established), the moment will come when we are complete.

I've taken the time to quote these biblical passages, because I want to establish by the Bible, that there are no exceptions to this rule. NO ONE CAN ESCAPE the process that GOD has established for them. You only hand out tracts? This includes you! Even though our conversion was miraculous, and it definitely was, this does not mean that we are now ready. GOD has not prepared US as alternate "Christ's" to save souls, resolve problems, bring peace to the World, cause the desert to flourish, and bring abundance to the poor. NO! There's a process of time and testing that you have to go through, before GOD is done with you, SO THAT the **ONLY CHRIST** will be revealed <u>through you</u>.

Some of us think that because we are now the sons of GOD, we can eliminate the divine steps that even the foolish world instinctively uses every day to attain success with their goods. Because JESUS was the Son of GOD, could HE eliminate the requirements of the Law? NO. The Bible says that HE came to fulfill the law (that HE Himself established). After HE was obedient even unto death, was when the FATHER gave HIM Power and Authority over the world and everything in the world.

Without the trials (tests, critiques, stresses, problems, evaluations, fire, etc.), with the accompanying passage of time, and the FINAL APPROVAL OF GOD, we run the risk of becoming defective products, full of errors, legalists, enslaved, and the discarded proud. These are products that the Almighty GOD has NOT APPROVED or RELEASED for HIS use. Instead, these defective and oftentimes dangerous "products" come from the flesh and the devil. GOD has no use for it, except to throw it into the fire.

Thank GOD for the trials that He sends us! Okay, I said it! Can you say it? Again, thank GOD for the trials that He sends us! As Bishop John Gimenez used to say, "We need to go thru the necessary things." Although we can't prevent the winds or the waves, we've learned that in those stormy days, **ONLY THE THINGS THAT WE HAVE NOT SUBMITTED TO THE SOVEREIGNTY OF GOD ARE LOST.** All that we give to GOD remains with us.

Is it possible, dear reader, that there are still a few things that you need to go through before you're able to teach the perfect truths of GOD, with the authority that comes from GOD HIMSELF? Well, don't be too concerned. As I mentioned earlier, GOD IS COMING TO COMPLETE THE WORK HE STARTED IN YOU! In the meantime, give yourself to GOD, study the Word, meditate on the outlines in this book, and ask the Father for Wisdom. Soon, GOD will cause your Pastor or the Sunday school teacher to begin to use you in the LORD'S vineyard. Don't worry, they won't ask you to do what you're not ready to do yet, but they will send you where they most need you. GOD knows that we the Pastors and Teachers need all the help that we can get. Just be ready to serve. GOD will MAKE YOU GREAT as you serve.

To the pastors, their assistants, and the teachers that have already gone through a few courses at HOLY SPIRIT University (the PEA) – I say to you as Paul said to Timothy:

- 1 Timothy 6:20 *"O Timothy, Guard what was committed to your trust, avoiding the profane and idle babblings and contradictions of what is falsely called knowledge"*
- 2 Timothy 2:23 *"But avoid foolish and ignorant disputes, knowing that they generate strife."*
- 2 Timothy 4:2 *"Preach the word! Be ready in season and out of season. Convince, rebuke, exhort, with all longsuffering and teaching."*

I want to let the brethren know "you don't have to wait for The Lord to finish His work in you. Just willingly enter into the process of GOD." Start with Christianity 1-111 found in 1 Corinthians 11:1 "Imitate me, just as I also *imitate* Christ." GOD will make sure that you complete HIS process. Without a doubt, despite the hurts and bruises you'll get, you will graduate with honors. All you need to do is seek GOD from now on, with ALL of your soul, with ALL of your strength, and with ALL of your mind, and you will be ready to start teaching the Word, without placing any of your trust in your personal abilities, or knowledge, instead it will be in the strength that comes totally from GOD. Who knows? Seeking GOD with ALL you are might possibly save you a small bruise here and there.

The outlines that I present to you today were never meant to be exhaustive treatises on any of the presented topics. These outlines were also not written to touch on all the great biblical doctrines that we as Disciples of Christ should know. These outlines were not written to inflate my ego or so that I could have an outlet for pride. On the contrary, the idea that GOD gave me was and still is, to prepare spiritual appetizers for my family in Christ – so that they can taste and appreciate the divine food that GOD has prepared for HIS children. I give you these basic Bible teachings that we all need to have, know, and desire, as expressed in Hebrews 6:1, 2 as well as a few other GREAT truths that we should know after a few months in Christ, so as to strengthen our foundation in, and to mature in Christ. I expect and pray that your spiritual appetites will be opened, so that you will desire to enroll in the colleges, universities, and bible institutes that GOD has prepared, to strengthen the principles that have already begun to be established in our lives. ABOVE ALL it is under the direction of the HOLY SPIRIT, that we will become established and strengthened for the work that is still ahead of us. I pray that GOD will direct us (the pastors and leaders of the churches) as we choose people full of the HOLY SPIRIT, to help us teach the people of GOD, what is already high time that they knew. It is under the direction of the HOLY SPIRIT, that these teachers and leaders (chosen carefully by their pastors), will allow these studies to help and encourage everyone (no matter what their past may be), to understand and assimilate the most basic teachings of Scripture, so that they can confidently resist EVERY WAVE AND WIND that may come to buffet them, for THEY WILL KNOW that it is THE PROCESS OF GOD FOR THEIR LIVES.

In these days of so many advances around us – it is time that we get to the unity of the faith, and to mature – to demonstrate to the world and the devil that the time has come for the manifestation of the sons of GOD. Surely my brothers, we don't have time to waste in arguments, complaining about one another, criticizing one another, foolishly looking for new places to eat new foods (or divine revelations), or get ministry support, or to search for places where "GOD is moving" the way we want. NO! It is time for the CHURCH of GOD to awaken from its slumber, get dressed, and start walking to the wedding feast where the groom is waiting. It doesn't matter if the dressing room we've been assigned to is "frumpish" or "garish" or "too poor" not fitting OUR STYLE! Surprise, but <u>WE HAVE NO SAY IN THIS</u>! Wherever GOD has placed us, is where we belong! It is that place where YOU – not the rest of the congregation, has to finish getting ready! THE GROOM IS AT THE DOOR! GET READY! Get ready! GET READY!

I expect that the HOLY SPIRIT will lead you and teach you the truth of HIS WORD. It is my desire that as we study and begin to teach these truths, that we will avoid those areas of controversy that separate us. It is also my desire that we will also avoid those areas that cause our flesh to stir, that cause our hairs to stand on end, and which allow pride to enter in. IN THE NAME OF JESUS, I pray that those areas of strife, disagreement, and of ego that cause us to boldly walk in the FLESH, so as to break apart churches, hurt people, and try to remove the pastor will even now be destroyed! I command those strongholds of hell to even now BE BROKEN, in The NAME OF JESUS!

My brothers, by the authority of the Word of GOD, and by the direction of the HOLY SPIRIT, I charge all the Teachers, Pastors, Evangelists, Missionaries, Administrators, Prophets, and children of GOD, to use these study outlines to unite and encourage the brethren from the church. Use these studies so that we can all speak the same, pray the same, think the same, and teach the same, so that the HOLY SPIRIT will allow us – the church - to finally reach a unity of the faith, and the measure of the stature of the perfect man – JESUS CHRIST.

Let's focus on teaching the basic truths of the Bible (perhaps they're boring to those with "itching ears" or to the world or to the flesh BUT in the eternal universe of GOD, and to us, it is THE ETERNAL, IMMUTABLE WORD OF GOD). We desperately need the "old way" of seeking for GOD, so as to become useful servants of GOD. Even as the great revivalist and preacher – Rev. Dr. Howard O. Jameson, used to preach during the time I was still a very young man and he was evangelizing the world in his outdoor gospel tents "If it's new it's not true, and if it's true, it's not new!" and he would proceed to present Jesus Christ as the Savior and Lord of the Church! The Bible says in *1 John 2:16 "For all that is in the world—the lust of the flesh, the lust of the eyes, and the pride of life—is not of the Father but is of the world."* We don't want the mess that is in the world. We don't want whatever current fashion or intellectual wave is passing by. As I know Dr. Jameson would surely say "WE WANT WHAT IS ESTABLISHED AND TRUE. WE WANT JESUS!"

Even as the Lord Jesus did, let us resist the temptations that will show up in our path, and if you somehow missed the class that I previously mentioned (Christianity 1-111), today you will begin that class. READ THE FOLLOWING OUT LOUD: *"I will be an imitator of Jesus Christ, even as the Apostle Paul was."* ALSO READ THIS OUT LOUD A FEW TIMES: *"I will not allow anything to stop me from preaching the Gospel to the entire World. HOLY SPIRIT I ask that YOU fill me with the life of Christ. I promise that I will leave everything that the world and the flesh can offer me. Thank you FATHER, because I have been grafted into the Vineyard of Jesus. Thank you LORD because with your help I will produce much fruit. Thank you GOD, because with your help I will know how to produce genuine disciples of Christ."*

As we move into our study series, our life of Bible study begins with the following warning (read it a few times till it sinks in):

"<u>WITHOUT THE TESTING OF GOD</u> *(to see what decisions you will make in your life – that's your spirit, soul, and body - or in other words: in your emotions; in your intellect; in your sub-conscious thoughts; in your self-control; in your purity; in your living sacrifice; in handling your temptations; in managing your spiritual battles; in your obedience to the HOLY SPIRIT),* <u>YOU CAN ONLY BECOME A CARNAL ZOMBIE FULL OF TRADITION, DEAD LETTERS, AND HATRED</u>. You will be incomplete and fleshly, but don't worry, that's NOT GODS PLAN FOR YOU. If you love HIM, get ready, get ready, GET READY! <u>HE'S GOING TO GET YOU READY!</u>

I conclude this introduction with a quote from Ephesians 4:1-14

[1]*I, therefore, the prisoner of the Lord, beseech you to walk worthy of the calling with which you were called,* [2]*with all lowliness and gentleness, with longsuffering, bearing with one another in love,* [3]*endeavoring to keep the unity of the Spirit in the bond of peace.* [4]*There is one body and one Spirit, just as you were called in one hope of your calling;* [5]*one Lord, one faith, one baptism;* [6]*one GOD and Father of all, who is above all, and through all, and in* [£]*you all.*
[7]*But to each one of us grace was given according to the measure of Christ's gift.* [8]*Therefore He says:*
"When He ascended on high, He led captivity captive, and gave gifts to men."
[9]*(Now this, "He ascended"—what does it mean but that He also first descended into the lower parts of the earth?* [10]*He who descended is also the One who ascended far above all the heavens, that He might fill all things.)* [11]*And He Himself gave some to be apostles, some prophets, some evangelists, and some pastors and teachers,* [12]*for the equipping of the saints for the work*

of ministry, for the edifying of the body of Christ, ¹³till we all come to the unity of the faith and of the knowledge of the Son of GOD, to a perfect man, to the measure of the stature of the fullness of Christ; ¹⁴that we should no longer be children, tossed to and fro and carried about with every wind of doctrine, by the trickery of men, in the cunning craftiness of deceitful plotting..."

Amen. I give this book to You Lord, with all my heart.

Rev. Aramis Torres, DD

LESSONS

OUTLINE

I. The Plan of Salvation
  A. Word Definitions
    1. Define the word salvation.
      Def.: To be delivered from something, to avoid something, to escape something
    2. Define the word sin?
      Def.: Disobey, transgress, or ignore the commands of GOD.
    3. What is a sinner?
      Def.: One who breaks, disobeys, or ignores GODS commands
      a. Even "good people" have disobeyed GODS law
      b. Decent & noble people in society, without thinking break laws like "cross only when the Light is green."

II. In the Beginning
  A. Man is created without sin by GOD. Genesis 1 & 2
    1. Man was perfect
  B. GOD gave man a command. Genesis 2:15-17
    1. Transgressing GODS commands is sin.
      Genesis 3:6; Galatians 2:18; James 2:11
  C. The result of sin is death. Genesis 3:17-19, 24
    1. What is death?
      Def.: Separation from the source of life. Isaiah 59:1, 2; Ezekiel 18:20; Romans 5:12

III. Who is a sinner?

LESSON# 1	TOPIC: SALVATION
(continued)	Romans 5; John 3

OUTLINE

III. Who is a sinner?
    A. All. Isaiah 53:6; Romans 3:10-12, 23
    B. Sin entered the World through ADAM; Salvation from our sins through Jesus. Romans 5:8, 9
        1. The law demanded a penalty for the transgressor. Ezekiel 18:4, 20
           a. ADAM died. Genesis 3:24, 5:5
           b. JESUS died. Isaiah 53:5; Hebrews 9:22, 27, 28; Romans 5:18, 19, 6:10
        2. The debt is paid in full. John1:29; Leviticus 17:11; Hebrews 5:8, 9, 9:22

IV. Man's Salvation – The Plan of GOD. John3:16, 17 Hebrews 5:9
    A. The Plan of Salvation in the Bible
        1. Promised at the beginning. Genesis 3:15
        2. Announced to Abraham. Genesis 12:1-3; Galatians 3:8, 9
        3. Promised to Israel. Zechariah9:9
        4. Revealed to the Prophets. 1 Peter 1:10-12
        5. Promised to the Gentiles. Isaiah 45:22
        6. Accomplished and realized by the Messiah. Isaiah 59:16, 17; 9:6; Luke 2:8-11
        7. Rejected by Israel. Acts 13:26-46
        8. Presented to the Gentiles. Acts 10:28-35, 28:28
        9. The Church is the day of Salvation. 2 Corinthians 6:1, 2
    B. The source of Salvation is Christ. Acts 4:12; Hebrews 7:25
        1. Given by the grace and love of GOD. Ephesians 2:4, 5, 8; John 3:16; Romans 5:8

LESSON# 1	TOPIC: SALVATION
(continued)	Romans 5; John 3

OUTLINE

V. What do I need to do to be saved? Acts 16:31
   A. Salvation – The gift received by FAITH. Ephesians 2:8
      1. FAITH – the decision to OBEY GOD. 1 Kings 18:36

VI. The components of SAVING FAITH. John 3:3, 5; Acts 2:38; 1 John 5:8
   A. REPENT & CONVERT (to admit and change your direction or path).
      1. This is an old topic. Psalms 1:1; 34:14, 18; Proverbs 1:22, 23; 28:13
         a. This is granted by GOD. 2 Timothy 2: 24-26
         b. It is a cause for JOY IN HEAVEN. Luke 15:1-24
      2. Repent from DEAD WORKS (works without faith). Mark 1:15; Luke 13:3-5, 18:20-22
         a. I give to the poor, the Church, I don't kill, etc. Hebrews 11:6
      3. CONFESS (say, speak, declare). Matthew 10:32, Acts 2:21; Romans 10:8-10; 1 John 1:9
   B. RECEIVE (welcome in) Jesus. John 1:12, 13, 6:37
      1. OBEY His commands. John 14:15, 23; 15:10
      2. BELIEVE. Acts 16:30, 31
         a. As a teaching tool, I like to define this word as "Know" so as to differentiate it from the weak and tepid word used in our world system. "I believe I saw them," by this meaning that they could have been right but they could have been wrong. Therefore I teach that when we say "I believe in Jesus Christ as my Savior, we mean "I KNOW Jesus Christ as my Savior.

LESSON# 1	TOPIC: SALVATION
(continued)	Proverbs 18:21; Romans 5; John 3

OUTLINE

    C. PERFORM living Works. James 1:22; 2:14, 17-22
       1. Works that reflect our FAITH. Hebrews 11:6
       2. "I'm going to this so they won't talk." or "I'm going to do that so that they'll be impressed." This is NOT FAITH.
    D. HAVE YOU BELIEVED & RECEIVED JESUS CHRIST AS YOUR SAVIOUR?
       1. If you haven't, today is the day GOD'S chosen for you to be saved.

VII. The Law of Witnesses - Deuteronomy 19:15; Matthew 18:16; 2 Corinthians 13:1
    A. But how do we know we're saved? <u>Because there are witnesses.</u>
       1. First – it is written. Matthew 10:32; Luke 12:8; Romans 10:9; 1 John 3:14, 21-24; 4:15
       2. Second – Because we obey His commandments. John14:15; 1 John 3:6, 8-10
       3. Third – GOD Himself has established witnesses: The Blood of Jesus, Water Baptism, & His HOLY SPIRIT. 1 John 5:8

Discussion Questions & Thoughts

1. Now, what is the definition of Salvation for you?
2. Can you feel Salvation? NO. (To believe is an act of Faith!)
3. Although saved, can I continue in sin? NO! Romans 6:1-11; 1 John 1:5-6
4. Okay, but what if I do sin? 1 John 1:9
5. What can I do when I remember things that I did and I feel guilty for those things?

LESSON# 1   TOPIC: SALVATION

(continued)   Proverbs 18:21; Romans 5; John 3

OUTLINE

Discussion Questions & Thoughts *(continued)*

6. I've heard that once I become born again I should return everything I've ever stolen from anyone. Is this true?
7. I was told that if I didn't get baptized immediately (this is a Word that is used extensively in the gospel of Mark) I was not saved yet, and I was destined be lost. I haven't been baptized yet. The church I go to has specific days that they baptize, and other churches don't even have a baptistery! If I wait, am I in sin? Am I not saved?

LESSON# 2   TOPIC: WATER BAPTISM

READING: Mark 16:16; John 3; 1 John 5

<u>OUTLINE</u>

I. You must be BORN AGAIN!
   A. NICODEMUS. John 3:1-18
      1. Be BAPTIZED! Mark 16:16; Acts 2:37, 38
      2. We are born of WATER & THE SPIRIT. John 3:5
   B. Who should be BAPTIZED?
      1. THE BELIEVER. Acts 2:41, 18:8
         a. Infant baptism is not practiced in the Bible. (How can they use their FAITH?)
      2. It is a COMMAND for the believer.
         a. By Christ. Matthew 28:19, 20; Mark 16:16
         b. Baptism in water is in the NAME of the FATHER, the SON, & the HOLY SPIRIT.
            i. And what is this name? JESUS!! Philippians 2:9; Acts 4:12; John 10:30, 14:7, 9
         c. Baptism was done by the disciples. Acts 2:38, 10:46-48

II. THE NEW BIRTH!!
   A. This is a DIVINE process
      1. By the HOLY SPIRIT. John 3:5, 8; Titus 3:5
      2. By THE WORD. Ephesians 5:25-27; James 1:18; 1 Peter 1:23
      3. By our OBEDIENCE. John 5:24; 8:51; 14:23
   B. A new CREATION. 2 Corinthians 5:17; 1 Peter 1:3
      1. Our LIVES are CHANGED. Romans 6:4-11; 1 John 3:10, 5:4
      2. The control of our life is now in the hands of the HOLY SPIRIT. Romans 8:14
         a. Now, by the SPIRIT, we obey GOD & we demonstrate the fruits of the SPIRIT. Galatians 5:16-18

LESSON# 2   TOPIC: WATER BAPTISM

(continued)   Mark 16:16; John 3; 1 John 5

<u>OUTLINE</u>

III. Our OBEDIENCE to THE WORD confirms our FAITH
    A. We are saved by FAITH. Ephesians 2:4, 5, 7, 8
    B. We walk by FAITH, not by sight 2 Corinthians 5:7
        1. We are free from the slavery of SIN. Matthew 1:21
        2. We are free from the power of the devil. Hebrews 2:14, 15
        3. We are free from the WRATH of GOD. Romans 5:9
        4. We are free from the eternal death. John 3:16, 17
    C. We now have RESPONSIBILITY!
        1. Work! (Our WORKS) Mark 16:15; James 2:14-26; John 3:14

IV. We are baptized. Mark 16:16
    A. Characteristics of water baptism.
        1. SUBMERSION. Acts 8:38, 10:47; Galatians 3:27; Romans 6:4, 5
        2. There is ONLY ONE BAPTISM. Ephesians 4:4, 5, 6
        3. It is NECESSARY. Acts 2:38, 41

V. Define submersion in water
    A. Submersion in water is FIGURATIVE of the burial and resurrection of CHRIST. Romans 6:3-4; Galatians 3:27; Colossians 2:12-13
    B. It is FIGURATIVE of the new birth. John 3:3, 5, 6; Romans 6:3, 4, 11

VI. Are you baptized?
    A. Jesus said "If you love me, obey my commandments." John 14:15

LESSON# 2	TOPIC: WATER BAPTISM
(continued)	Mark 16:16; John 3; 1 John 5

OUTLINE

Discussion Questions & Thoughts

1. When should I get baptized? (The Bible teaches us to do it as soon as possible. Acts 2:41, 8:35-37, 10:47, 16:33)
2. My baptism as a baby is it valid or do I have to be baptized again? (The Bible teaches us that children were blessed by their parents, and that they were also dedicated to the Lord, but it does not say that they would baptize them. We need to think – How are they able to express their faith?)
3. Is there a minimum age in order to be baptized? (Although the Bible does tell us about our children's education, it does not give us a specific age at which they should be baptized. Now on the contrary, BELIEVING is the ONLY REQUIREMENT – SEE Acts 8:37 – Although many congregations have utilized a cutoff of 12 years old as the minimum age that they will baptize someone, it is only a TRADITION. We can understand why this may be so, since as parents we are sometimes pushy with our kids to do what we think is for their benefit. This can cause us to not understand that they have to believe for themselves.)

LESSON# 3   TOPIC: THE HOLY SPIRIT

READING: John 14; 15:26-27, 16:7-16; Acts 2

OUTLINE

I. The person of the HOLY SPIRIT
  A. GOD
    1. Called GOD. Acts 5:3, 4
    2. With the FATHER and SON. Matthew 28:19; 2 Corinthians 13:14
    3. Attributes of the HOLY SPIRIT (characteristics)
      a. ETERNAL. Hebrews 9:14
      b. OMNIPOTENT. Luke 1:35
      c. OMNISCIENT. I Corinthians 2:10, 11
      d. OMNIPRESENT. Psalms 139:7-12
  B. Attributes of a PERSON is assigned by the Bible
    1. Speaks. Acts 28:25
    2. Teaches. John 14:26
    3. Contends with man. Genesis 6:3
    4. Strengthens. Acts 9:31
    5. Helps us with our weaknesses. Romans 8:26
    6. Can be grieved. Ephesians 4:30
    7. Can be resisted. Acts 7:51

II. The promise of the SPIRIT
  A. The promise is given to His people. Joel 2:28-32; John 14:16-18; Acts 1:8
  B. The promise if fulfilled. Acts 2:1-21, 10:45

III. The CHURCH is formed
  A. Established by JESUS. Matthew 16:18

LESSON# 3	TOPIC: THE HOLY SPIRIT
(continued)	John 14; 15:26-27, 16:7-16; Acts 2

OUTLINE

B. Anointed by the SPIRIT. Acts 2:1-4

IV. The work of the SPIRIT
  A. The HOLY SPIRIT in the ministry of CHRIST
    1. Conception. Matthew 1:18; Luke 1:35
    2. Miracles. Matthew 12:28
    3. Anointing. Matthew 3:16; Isaiah 61:1
    4. Fill & help. Luke 4:1, 17, 18
    5. Offered to GOD by the Spirit. Hebrews 9:14
    6. Is raised from the dead. Romans 1:4
    7. Justified by the Spirit. 1 Timothy 3:16
  B. THE HOLY SPIRIT in the believers
    1. Regenerates us. John 3:3, 5
    2. Is in us. Romans 8:11
    3. Baptizes us. Acts 2; Isaiah 44:3; John 1:32, 33
    4. Guides us. John 16:13
    5. Gives us power. Acts 1:8
    6. Sanctifies us. Romans 15:16; 2 Thessalonians 2:13
    7. Is a witness. Romans 8:16; Hebrews 10:15
    8. Our Helper. John 14:16-26
    9. Our justice, peace, & joy. Romans 14:17
    10. Discernment. 1 Corinthians 2:10-16
    11. Gives gifts. I Corinthians 12:3-11
    12. Brings fruit. Galatians 5:22, 23
    13. Teaches. John14:26
    14. Reveals what is GOD. Isaiah 40:13; 1 Corinthians 2:9-13

LESSON# 3   TOPIC: THE HOLY SPIRIT

(continued)   John 14; 15:26-27, 16:7-16; Acts 2

OUTLINE

    C. The HOLY SPIRIT in the Church
        1. Baptizes. 1 Corinthians 12:13
        2. Fills. Acts 2:4
        3. Chooses Leaders. Acts 20:28
        4. Separates for the Ministry. Acts 13:2, 4
        5. Leads ministers. Acts 8:29
        6. Strengthens. Acts 9:31

Discussion Questions & Thoughts

1. Who can receive the HOLY SPIRIT? (Believers in Jesus – Acts 2:37-39)
2. Some say if we don't speak in tongues we don't have the HOLY SPIRIT. Is this true? (NO! The baptism in the HOLY SPIRIT is a singular and unique experience, different from receiving direction, guidance, and being sealed after being born again. Although the baptism is known by the manifestation of speaking in tongues, this has nothing to do with the gifts of the SPIRIT. The gifts come from the SPIRIT but the SPIRIT is for every believer. Luke 11:11-13; 1 Corinthians 12:1, 4-13)
3. Is the baptism in the HOLY SPIRIT for children also? (Like water baptism, the only requirement is to believe.)

LESSON# 4   TOPIC: FAITH IN GOD
  READING: Hebrews 11; James 1

OUTLINE

I. FAITH – the classic definition. Hebrews 11:1
  A. Obedience to the Word of GOD. 1 Kings 18:36

II. By FAITH we have victory. Habakkuk 2:4; 1 John 5:4; Galatians 5:6
  A. Classes of FAITH
    1. FAITH that does not weaken. Romans 4:19, 20
    2. Great FAITH. Matthew 8:5-10
    3. FAITH that grows. 2 Thessalonians 1:3
    4. FAITH as a GRAIN of Mustard. Matthew 17:20; Luke 17:6
    5. Steadfastness of FAITH. Colossians 2:5

III. FAITH – The WORK of GOD. John 6:28, 29
  A. Believe. John 3:16, 17, 11:25, 26
  B. FAITH that pleases GOD. Hebrews 11:6
    1. FAITH without doubt. James 1:5-7; Matthew 8:13, 9:29
    2. FAITH without limits. Matthew 17:20; Mark 9:23
      a. Get all the FAITH you need. Romans 10:17

IV. FAITH in action
  A. Word of FAITH. Romans 10:8
    1. What you say is important. Numbers 14:28; Proverbs 18:20, 21; 2 Corinthians 4:13
      a. FAITH comes by HEARING GOD. Romans 10:17
      b. The word of FAITH is in YOUR MOUTH. Romans 10:10; Matthew 17:20
  B. Prayer of FAITH.
    1. Your prayer is also by FAITH. James 1:6, 5:15

LESSON# 4   TOPIC: FAITH IN GOD

(continued)   Hebrews 11; James 1

<u>OUTLINE</u>

Discussion Questions & Thoughts

1. What is Faith? (Knowing what GOD says in HIS Word is more real than the life around us.)
    a. FAITH is obedient to the Word of GOD. (Examine the heroes of Hebrews 11).
    b. The WORD is our GUIDE. Romans 10:17
2. Can you have FAITH without uttering a single word? NO! Matthew 12:34.35, Romans 10:10
3. How can you get more faith? (Faith comes by hearing.)

LESSON# 5   TOPIC: JESUS OF NAZARETH, THE MESSIAH
READING: Isaiah 53; John 6, 20; Matthew 28; Mark 16; Luke 24;
1Corinthians 15

<u>OUTLINE</u>

I. Jesus the LAMB of GOD. John 1:29
   A. The Savior. Luke 2:11; John 3:17; 1 Timothy 1:15; Hebrews 7:25
   B. The Just dies for the unjust. Isaiah 53:5, 6; Matthew 27; Luke 23:46; 1 Peter3:18; Hebrews 2:9
   C. He bore our sins. Hebrews 9:28; 1 Peter 2:24; Isaiah 53:12

II. He died for our sins, but death COULD NOT HOLD HIM!
   A. Like HIS BIRTH, HIS RESURRECTION was announced by angels. Matthew 28:2-6; Mark 16:5, 6; Luke 24:4, 6
   B. There were witnesses for HIS RESURRECTION
      1. His disciples. Acts 1:1-3, 3:14-15, 10:39-41
      2. Many others. Matthew 28:9, 17; Luke 24:15, 36, 50; John 20:19, 26, 21:1; 1 Corinthians 15:5-8
   C. He was RECEIVED ON HIGH! Acts 1:1, 2, 9-11
      1. He is SEATED at the RIGHT HAND OF GOD and is EXALTED. Mark 16:19; Ephesians 1:19-22; Philippians 2:9-11

III. He lives forevermore!
   A. Alfa & Omega. Revelation 1:8, 22:13
   B. Lord & King. 1 Corinthians 8:6; 15:25; Philippians 2:9-11; Colossians 1:12-20; Hebrews 10:12-13
   C. He's coming again. Acts 1:9-11

IV. Jesus, THE SON of GOD. John 1:33, 34
   A. The manifestation of GOD. John1:1
      1. Made flesh. John 1:14
      2. Thomas declares who Jesus is. John 20:28

LESSON# 5   TOPIC: JESUS OF NAZARETH, THE MESSIAH

(continued):   Isaiah 53; John 6, 20; Matthew 28; Mark 16; Luke 24;
1Corinthians 15

OUTLINE

IV. Jesus, THE SON of GOD. John 1:33, 34 (Continued)
    3. He HIMSELF declares who HE is. Revelation 1:8, 10, 11-17
  B. Some of HIS MINISTRIES
    1. Our SAVIOUR. Acts 2:21; 1 Corinthians 6:9-11; Acts 16:30, 31
    2. Our INTERCESOR & MEDIATOR. Hebrews 7:25; 8:6; 12:24
    3. Our REST. Matthew 11:28-30
    4. THE AUTHOR & FINISHER of our faith. Hebrews 12:2
    5. THE BREAD of LIFE. John 6:35
    6. Our COUNSELOR. Isaiah 9:6
    7. Our DELIVERER. Romans 11:26
    8. Our DOOR to GOD. John 10:2, 7
    9. Our FRIEND. Luke 7:34
    10. Our HIGH PRIEST. Hebrews 4:14
    11. Our HUSBAND. 2 Corinthians 11:2
    12. THE WAY THE TRUTH THE LIFE. John 14:6
    13. Our PEACE. Ephesians 2:14
    14. Our PHYSICIAN (Spirit, soul & body). Luke 4:23; Isaiah 61:1
    15. Our FOUNDATION. 1 Corinthians 3:11
    16. The CORNERSTONE. Isaiah 28:16; 1 Peter 2:6
    17. Our RESURECTION. John 11:25
    18. THE ROCK. 1 Corinthians 10:4
    19. Our GOOD SHEPHERD. John 10:11
    20. Our LAWYER. 1John 2:1
    21. Our LORD. Philippians 2:9-11; Philippians

LESSON# 5   TOPIC: JESUS OF NAZARETH, THE MESSIAH

(continued):   Isaiah 53; John 6, 20; Matthew 28; Mark 16; Luke 24;
1Corinthians 15

OUTLINE

Discussion Questions & Thoughts

1. Should we be worried about our past sins? (Do we worry about debts that have been paid-off?)
2. If we sin, is everything lost or is forgiveness available? 1 John 1:9
3. How does marriage affect our lives? Isn't this how the Lord is with us?
4. What is the importance of the resurrection?
5. How should this affect you?
6. Three steps in our growth in the gospel.
    a. Is Jesus your Savior?
    b. Is Jesus your Lord?
    c. Is Jesus your Friend?

LESSON# 6   TOPIC: PRAYER

READING: Matthew 6:5-18; Luke 11:1-28; 18:1-14

OUTLINE

I. Prayer – Communicating with GOD.
   A. Why PRAY? Matthew 7:7-11, 26:41
      1. It delights the Lord. Proverbs 15:8
      2. As INCENSE before GOD. Psalms 141:2; Revelation 5:8, 8:4

II. A Biblical outline.
   A. At what time should we Schedule prayer? Daniel 6:10
      1. Morning. Mark 1:35; Psalms 55:17
      2. Noon. Psalms 55:17
      3. Night. 1 Samuel 15:11; Luke 6:12; Psalms 55:17
   B. Should we pray three times a day?
      1. Always. Ephesians 6:18; Luke 18:1; 1 Thessalonians 5:17
      2. In times of anguish. Psalms 118:5
      3. In affliction. James 5:13

III. In what manner should we PRAY?
   A. A partial list
      1. In the name of JESUS. John 16:24
      2. Following the example of CHRIST. Matthew 6:7-13
      3. Believing & Forgiving. Mark 11:24-26; Matthew 6:14
      4. In the SPIRIT. Romans 8:26; Ephesians 6:18
      5. Humbling ourselves & confessing our SINS. 2 Chronicles 7:14
      6. With all our HEART. Jeremiah 29:13
      7. With WORSHIP. Daniel 4:34, 35
      8. Making INTERCCESION. James 5:14, 15
      9. With THANKSGIVING. Philippians 4:6
      10. According to the WILL of GOD. 1 John 5:14
      11. Simply. Matthew 6:5, 6

LESSON# 6   TOPIC: PRAYER

(continued)   Matthew 6:5-18; Luke 11:1-28; 18:1-14

<u>OUTLINE</u>

   A. A partial list (continued)
       12. With TENACITY. Luke 11:5-8, 18:1-8
       13. With INTENSITY. Matthew 7:7-11

IV. What should we PRAY for?
   A. A PARTIAL list of prayers
       1. Using the template Jesus gave us. Matthew 6:9-13; Luke
          11:1-13
       2. For our government. 1 Timothy 2:1, 2
       3. To receive the HOLY SPIRIT. Luke 11:13
       4. Wisdom. James 1:5
       5. For boldness. Acts 4:24-31
       6. For prosperity. 3 John 2
       7. One for another. 1 Thessalonians 5:25

V. Various types of prayer
   A. A PARTIAL list
       1. In secret. Matthew 6:6
       2. With the family. Acts 10:2, 30
       3. As a group. Matthew 18:20; Acts 4:24, 31
       4. In public. 1 Corinthians 14:14-17
       5. In agreement. Matthew 18:19

VI. Will you be answered? Psalms 99:6; John 15:7; 1 John 3:22; 5:14-
    15
   A. The Bible says it will be according to your FAITH. Mark
      11:24
   B. Once again Tenacity also seems to play an important part but
      this may be a by-product of your faith. . Luke 11:5-8, 18:1-8

LESSON# 6   TOPIC: PRAYER

(continued)   Matthew 6:5-18; Luke 11:1-28; 18:1-14

OUTLINE

VII. What can impede our prayers?
   A. Sin. Psalms 66:18
   B. If we ask incorrectly or with doubt. James 1:5-7; 4:3
   C. Pride. Luke 18:11, 12
   D. Disobedience. Proverbs 28:9
   E. Lack of wisdom or honor towards our spouses. 1 Peter 3:7
   F. Unforgiveness. Matthew 5:23, 24; 18:21-35

VIII. Is there a specific posture to pray?
   A. Don your knees. Ezra 9:5; Daniel 6:10
   B. Standing. Nehemiah 9:5
   C. Sitting. 1 Chronicles 17:16-27
   D. Bowed down. Exodus 34:8
   E. With hands upraised. 1 Timothy 2:8

Discussion Questions & Thoughts

1. Do you approach GOD boldly to pray? Hebrews 4:16
   a. By boldly we mean with the "confidence" of a child approaching
      their parents – NOT disrespectfully.
2. Can we pray about some things and hide others from GOD?
3. When should we pray?
4. Should we pray at least one hour?

LESSON# 7   TOPIC: NEW LIFE IN CHRIST

READING: John 3; Colossians 3; Romans 6; 1 John 5

OUTLINE

I. A new life (the old passed away). John 3:1-5; 2 Corinthians 5:17
   A. A new life in CHRIST is for all. 1 Corinthians 3:10, 11; Matthew
      28:18-20
      1. Based on the GOSPEL. 1 Corinthians 15:1-4
   B. Change is produced. 1 Corinthians 6:9-11
      1. We don't practice SIN. Isaiah 55:7; John 5:14; Romans6:11-14;
         Hebrews 12:1
      2. There's SELF CONTROL. 1 Peter 2:2, 11; Galatians 5:23;
         James 1:26, 27, 3:2-13
      3. Our CONDUCT with man. John 13:34, 35; Romans 14:13,
         18, 19
         a. Our CONDUCT with GOD. Matthew 22:36,37;
            Hebrews 11:6; 12:10,14; Philippians 2:4-11; 1 John 1:3

II. NEW LIFE
    A. Described:
       1. New Birth. John 1:13; 3:3, 5
       2. NEW CREATURES. 2 Corinthians 5:17
       3. We have a NEW HEART. Ezekiel 36:26
       4. Food is provided. Psalms 19:9, 10; 1 Peter 2:2, 3
       5. We have new clothes. Isaiah 61:10
       6. A life of growth. 2 Peter 3:18
       7. No longer in Darkness but in LIGHT. Matthew 5:16
       8. A LIFE of WISDOM (we're not moved). Matthew 7:24-27
       9. A LIFE of LIBERTY. John 8:31-32
       10. Members of the FAMILY of GOD. Ephesians 2:19-22
       11. We reflect the FATHER. 2 Corinthians 3:18
       12. We have a personal TUTOR. John 14:26
       13. We are jealous for good works. Titus 2:14

LESSON# 7   TOPIC: NEW LIFE IN CHRIST
(continued)   John 3; Colossians 3; Romans 6; 1 John 5

OUTLINE

II. NEW LIFE
   A. Described (continued):
      14. Producing FRUIT. John 15:1-6
      15. OBEDIENT. Philippians 2:12; 2 Thessalonians 1:8

Discussion Questions & Thoughts

1. The measure for our daily life is CHRIST. Should we measure ourselves frequently?
2. Are you becoming filled with the life of CHRIST? This happens only when you let CHRIST live in your life.
3. Do you realize that there have been changes in your life, compared to before you gave yourself to Christ?
4. Do you find that you have more self-control?
5. Have you noticed any increase in your patience?

LESSON# 8   TOPIC: THE BIBLE

READING: Psalms 119; 2 Timothy 3; 2 Peter 1:19-21

OUTLINE

I. The inspired Word of GOD. 2 Peter 1:19-21; 2 Timothy 3:12-17
   A. Names for THE BIBLE: The WORD OF GOD. Hebrews 4:12
      1. Book of THE LAW. Nehemiah 8:3 or Book: Revelation 22:19;
      2. THE LAW of GOD. Psalms 1:2
      3. The HOLY SCRIPTURES. John 5:39; Romans 1:2
      4. The WORD: James 1:21-23
      5. The WORD of LIFE. Philippians 2:16
   B. Described as:
      1. Perfect & pure. Psalms 19:7, 8
      2. Restraining us from sin. Psalms 119:11
      3. Sure. Psalms 111:7, 8
      4. True. Psalms 119:142, 151, 160
      5. Eternal. Isaiah 40:8
      6. Prosperous. Isaiah 55:11.
      7. Sanctified. Ephesians 5:26
      8. In agreement. Acts 15:15
      9. Living & powerful. Hebrews 4:12
      10. The Verb or Word. John 1:1
   C. Has the Capacity to:
      1. Heal. Psalms 107:20
      2. Set Free. John 8:32
      3. Illuminate. Psalms 119:130
      4. Produce Faith. John 20:31; Romans 10:17
      5. Make Wise. 2 Timothy 3:15-17

LESSON# 8   TOPIC: THE BIBLE

(continued)   Psalms 119; 2 Timothy 3; 2 Peter 1:19-21

<u>OUTLINE</u>

      6. Exhort. 2 Timothy 4:2
      7. Bring joy & gladness to the Heart. Jeremiah 15:16
      8. Make us the first fruits. James 1:18
  D. Our attitude towards THE WORD should be:
      1. Fear. Psalms 119:161
      2. Trembling. Isaiah 66:2, 5
      3. Declare it. Jeremiah 23:28; 2 Timothy 2:15
      4. Speak it with boldness. Acts 4:29, 31
      5. Receive it. Acts 11: 1
      6. Obey it. 1 Peter3:1
      7. Be doers of it. James 1:22, 23

II. We need to know what the WORD OF GOD says.
  A. Study THE WORD. 2 Timothy 2:15
      1. We receive WISDOM. 2 Timothy 3:15
      2. We will be PERFECTED & PREPARED. 2 Timothy 3:16, 17
      3. Peace comes through THE WORD. Psalms 119:165
      4. GOD judges us by THE WORD. John 12:48; Jeremiah 36
      5. Lawlessness without THE WORD. Hosea 4:6; Proverbs 29:18
      6. GOD prospers us by THE WORD. Joshua 1:8; Psalms 1:1-3
      7. THE SWORD GOD has given us. Ephesians 6:17; Psalms 119:9-11; Matthew 4:1-11,

III. How should we study THE WORD?
  A. Start with prayer. Psalms 19:18; John 16:13-15
  B. From an attitude of Love. Psalm 119:48
  C. Anticipate the quiet (night) times to think about the Word. Psalm 118:148

LESSON# 8   TOPIC: THE BIBLE

READING: Psalms 119; 2 Timothy 3; 2 Peter 1:19-21

OUTLINE

    D. Meditating on it (with Reverence & Thoughtfulness). Psalms 119:11

    E. Obeying THE WORD. James 1:22

    F. Letting THE HOLY SPIRIT guide us. John 14:26; 16:13-15

Discussion Questions & Thoughts

1. Should we read the Bible like any other book?
2. What does it mean to read the verses in context?"
3. Should I read many chapters every time I read the Bible?
4. Can GOD speak to me by the Scriptures?
5. Can I use Bible helps like "Bible Promises" or "Customs of The Bible" or "Systematic Theology of The Bible" or "Bible Concordance?" (It would probably be wise to speak with your Pastor or Sunday school Teacher before acquiring various Bible helps, since there are too many books with strange teachings or erroneous doctrines that are not useful to your Christian life.)
6. Why should I ask for wisdom to understand and read the Bible? (Much more important than any Bible guide is the help of the HOLY SPIRIT, who guides us to all truth.)

LESSON# 9	TOPIC: WHAT IS TRUTH?
READING:	John 18:38; 1 John 2:18-29, 4:1-13

<u>OUTLINE</u>

I. Liars and Lies. John 18:38
    A. A lie is defined in the Bible as:
        1. The nature of the devil. John 8:44
        2. Denying That JESUS is the CHRIST. 1 John 2:22
        3. Disobedience to commands of CHRIST. 1 John 2:4; 4:20
        4. Everything that is not truth. 1 John 2:21, 27
    B. Those that speak lies:
        1. The wicked. Psalms 58:3
        2. False witnesses. Proverbs 14:5, 25
        3. Astrologers. Daniel 2:9
        4. Grouped with the unjust and sinners. 1 Timothy 1:9-11
            a. Will eat the fruit of destruction. Hosea 10:15
    C. The attitude of the righteous towards lies:
        1. Stay away. Proverbs 30:8.
        2. Not speak lies. Zephaniah 3:13
        3. Pray for deliverance from sin. Psalms 120:2
        4. Puts away lies. Ephesians 4:25
    D. The attitude of GOD towards lies:
        1. He doesn't lie. Numbers 23:19
        2. Hates lies. Proverbs 6:16-19
        3. Reveals the lies of man. Isaiah 28:15, 17
        4. He's against lies. Ezekiel 13:8
    E. The evil of lies:
        1. Produces error. Amos 2:4

LESSON# 9   TOPIC: WHAT IS TRUTH?

(continued)   John 18:38; 1 John 2:18-29, 4:1-13

OUTLINE

E. The evil of lies (continued):
   2. Increases wickedness. Proverbs 29:12
   3. Brings destruction. Hosea 10:13-15
   4. Death. Proverbs 21:6; Zechariah 13:3
   5. Will burn in the lake of fire. Revelation 21:8

II. What is truth? John18:38, 39
   A. Truth is compared to:
      1. The LAW of GOD. Psalms 119:142-160
      2. CHRIST. John 14:6
      3. HOLY SPIRIT. John 14:17
      4. THE WORD of GOD. John 17:l7, 19
      5. THE GOSPEL. Galatians 2:5, 14
   B. Effects of truth:
      1. Makes us free. John 8:31, 32
      2. Sanctifies us. John 17:17-19
      3. Purifies us. 1 Peter 1:22
      4. Makes us grow. Ephesians 4:15

III. Do we need to differentiate between truth & lies? 1 Timothy 4:1-3, 6:3-5
   A. The devil knows the truth but twists it. Mark 1:24, 34; Luke 4:41; 2 Corinthians 11:1-4, 13, 15
   B. We need THE TRUTH (the complete counsel of GOD so as to not deviate from Him). John 8:32; Matthew 4:1-11; Psalms 119:11; 1 Corinthians 2:14; 1 Timothy 6:3-5

LESSON# 9   TOPIC: WHAT IS TRUTH?

(continued)   John 18:38; 1 John 2:18-29, 4:1-13

OUTLINE

IV. The Bible guides us to discern the truth.
    A. Test the spirits. 1 John 4:1-3; 1 Corinthians 12:3
        1. What are the motives? John 7:17; Galatians 1:8
        2. Observe the fruits. Matthew 3:8; Galatians 5:22, 23
        3 What is the attitude towards CHRIST? 1 John 2:21- 23
        4. What is the attitude towards the world? Romans 12:2
            a. Do we love the things of the world? 1 John 2:15
            b. Are we ensnared by them? (Physically, politically or mentally) 2 Timothy 2:4; 2 Peter 2:20
    B. What we hear is it in agreement with the BIBLE? Is it in context? 1 Timothy 6:3-5; 2 Peter 1:19-21; John 17:17

Discussion Questions & Thoughts

1. There are religions that deny that JESUS is the Son of GOD. Others say that He was only a man. Others say He was only a prophet. Others say that He did not resurrect from the dead. Others say that the Bible contains errors. Others say that in the original languages, Jesus was never presented as GOD. Should I pay attention to these arguments? Galatians 1:6-9
2. After reading John 7:17, 18 would you say that it is important to examine what our motives and those of our teachers are?

LESSON# 10   TOPIC: THE FAMILY

READING: Ephesians 5:22-32; Titus 2:1-8; 1 Peter 3:1-12

OUTLINE

I. The family is established
    A. The family is a divine creation. Genesis 1:27, 28
    B. Marriage (a physical and spiritual union). Matthew 19:3-6
        1. Instituted by GOD. Genesis 2:18-25
        2. Instruction of GOD. Genesis 1:26-28
           a. Multiply, rule, fill the earth
    C. The Bible view of family unity
        1. The spirit of the marriage is important. Malachi 2:13-16
        2. Unity of the parents. Exodus 20:12
        3. Unity of the parents & the children. Jeremiah 35:1-19
        4. Unity in congregational worship. 1 Corinthians 16:19
        5. Unity in Faith. 2 Timothy 1:5
        6. Unity in Baptism. Acts 16:31-33; Ephesians 4:5
        7. Unity in worship.
           a. Led by the dad. Genesis 18:19
           b. Taught in the Scriptures. Ephesians .6:4
    D. Disturbances to the family and marriage have to be avoided
        1. Polygamy. Genesis 4:19-24, 1 Samuel 1:2, 6, 7
        2. Lust. Genesis 34:1-31
        3. Jealousy. Genesis 37:3, 4, 18-27
        4. Lies. Genesis 37:31-35
        5. Hate. Genesis 4:5, 8
        6. Disputes. 2 Samuel 15:1-16
        7. Waste. Luke 15:11-18, 25-30
        8. Incredulity. John 7:1-9

LESSON# 10   TOPIC: THE FAMILY
(continued)   Ephesians 5:22-32; Titus 2:1-8; 1 Peter 3:1-12

OUTLINE

   9. The Works of the flesh. Galatians 5:19-21

II. The head of the family.
   A. The husband. Genesis 3:6; 1 Corinthians 11:3; Ephesians 5:23

III. Responsibilities of the husband & dad.
   A. Love. Genesis 37:4; Ephesians 5:25, 28, 33; 1 Corinthians 13,
   Colossians 3:19
     1. Provide for and care for the family. Ephesians 5:28-30
     2. Love without bitterness. Colossians 3:19
     3. Understand, respect, and honor the wife. 1 Peter 3:7
     4. Responsibility for what's promised. Numbers 30:13-15
     5. Teach & lead. Proverbs 1:8; 1 Thessalonians 2:11
     6. Not to provoke the children. Colossians 3:21
     7. To provide Discipline (structure). Hebrews12:7
     8. Supply the household needs. Matthew 7:8-11; 1 Timothy
     5:8
     9. Fulfill physical needs. 1 Corinthians 7:3, 4

IV. Responsibility of the wives and mothers
   A. Love. 1 Corinthians 13; 1 Peter3:8, Matthew 22:39
     1. Submit to proper authority. Ephesians 5:22-24; Colossians
     3:18; 1 Peter 3:1, 2
     2. Reverence (profound respect). Ephesians 5:33; 1 Peter 3:6
     3. Love the family and be discreet. Titus 2:3-5
     4. To be a helper in all. Genesis 2:18, 20, Proverbs 31:10-30

LESSON# 10   TOPIC: THE FAMILY

(continued0   Ephesians 5:22-32; Titus 2:1-8; 1 Peter 3:1-12

OUTLINE

IV. Responsibility of the wives and mothers (continued)
    5. Companionship. Malachi 2:14
    6. The wife must learn from the husband.
        a. The self sufficient were figuratively represented by Greece (Flesh). 1 Corinthians 14:34, 35; 1 Timothy 2:11-15
        b. The Christian woman was figuratively represented by Christ and Sara (Spiritual). Galatians 3:28; 1 Peter 3:1-4
    7. Be worthy of Trust. Proverbs 31:11, 12
    8. Fulfill physical needs. 1 Corinthians 7:3, 4

V. Responsibility of the children. Exodus 21:15, 17; Deuteronomy 30:2
  A. Love. 1 Corinthians 13
    1. Honor the parents. Ephesians 6:2, 3
    2. Obedience. Colossians 3:20; Ephesians 6:1
    3. Respect the elders. 1 Peter 5:5
    4. Take care of the parents. 1 Timothy 5:4
    5. Remember GOD. Ecclesiastes 12:1

VI. The perfect family. Matthew 6:33, 1 Corinthians 13; 1 John 3:1

Discussion Questions & Thoughts

1. "The Bible says the Woman has to submit." Talk about using an extremely minor section to develop a doctrine – of discrimination yet! This phrase has been used to enslave women for hundreds if not thousands of years. When is submission, in biblical context? Read Ephesians 4:1-3, 17-32; 5:1-30

LESSON# 11   TOPIC: CONTINUING IN CHRIST

READING: Hebrews 5:12 thru 6:3; 2 Peter 3:17-18

OUTLINE

I. Don't abuse your liberty in Christ. Romans 6:1, 2; 1 Corinthians
   8:1-13; 2 Corinthians 6:14-18, 7:1; Galatians 5:13-16

II. You need patience to:
    A. Attain the goal. Philippians 3:8-14, 4:8-14
    B. Receive from GOD. Psalms 27:14; John 3:27; James 1:17
    C. Finish. Hebrews 10:35-39, 12:1, 4; 2 Timothy 3:11-13

III. Seek the Kingdom first! Matthew 4:10, 6:33; Luke 10:27

IV. Flee vain discussions and arguments. Titus 3:9, 2 Timothy 2:22, 23

V. You're not defenseless. Ephesians 6:10, 11; 2 Timothy 1:7
   A. Our battle. Ephesians 6:12-17
      1. Use the Armor! Mark 16:15-18; Philippians 2:9-11
         a. Don't FEAR. Romans 14:8, 9; 1 Corinthians 15:54, 55
      2. Jesus is our rest. Matthew 11:27, 28

VI. GOD chose you! He'll give you what you need & keep you. John
    15:16; 16:23, 24; Romans 8:38, 39

VII. NEVER look back! Isaiah 30:20, 21; Luke 9:62; Philippians 3:13

VIII. The HOLY SPIRIT is in you! Psalms 51:10, 17; Isaiah 57:15;
      Romans 8:11

Discussion Questions & Thoughts

1. Have you been fighting within yourself, wondering if it really is worth
   all the difficulties that you're going through, just to follow Jesus?
   Revelation 2:11, 26, 27, 3:5
2. Christianity is not for wimps. How would you justify this
   statement?

LESSON# 11	TOPIC: CONTINUING IN CHRIST
(continued)	Hebrews 5:12 thru 6:3; 2 Peter 3:17-18

Discussion Questions & Thoughts (continued)

3. Do you feel like your strength is almost all gone? Perhaps you need to slow down just a little. There are times that we get filled with this great zeal motivating us, and perhaps just a little too quickly it begins to wear us out! It's nice to think that we can do this! Just a little more speed, just a little more effort, just a little more sacrifice, and we'll win this race! Wait a minute - this race is a marathon and NOT a short sprint! Listen to your pastors; to the teachers at your congregation, and; to the elders at your church, and above all listen to the HOLY SPIRIT that is in you. Can you hear Him? He's saying patience. Give it time. Remember: the crown is ONLY for those that FINISH THE RACE! Hebrews 10:35-39; 12:1-4

4. Should the failures of others cause you to be discouraged?

LESSON# 12   TOPIC: COMMUNION and CONGREGATION

READING: Hebrews 10:23-25; Acts 20:7; 1 Corinthians
                              11:18-34, 14:23-40, 16:1,2

OUTLINE

I. Fellowship. In Greek - KOINONIA (Communion, Sharing)
    A. This is important for the last days. Hebrews10:23-25

II. We get together to give and share. Acts 2:46
    A. Members should not be separated or isolated, or they'll die. 1
       Corinthians 12:12-27
    B. We can only share when we're together.
        1. The purpose we get together:
            a. Build ourselves. 1 Corinthians 14:4, 26; 1 Thessalonians
               5:11
            b. Fellowship. 1 John 1:1-3, 7
            c. Holy Communion & to receive the Word. Acts 20:7; 1
               Corinthians 11:23-34
            d. To give our offerings. 1 Corinthians 16:1, 2

III. Congregating together brings us closer to GOD. Psalms 133:1-3;
     Acts 2:42-47

IV. The result of fellowship.
    A. Fear of GOD with signs and wonders. Acts 2:42, 43
    B. Favor with the people. Acts 2:46, 47
    C. People will believe. Acts 2:1, 14, 37-41; John 17:20, 21
    D. The blessings of GOD flow. Psalms 133:1-3; Acts 2:1, 2, 4:31

Discussion Questions & Thoughts

1. Do you think GOD wants you to be alone by yourself, as a hermit?
2. Did GOD create TV ministry so that you could stay home?
3. I had a bad experience at one of the churches, "Can I stay home,
   watching Christian TV, and avoid becoming a member of a church?"

LESSON# 12   TOPIC: COMMUNION & CONGREGATION

(continued)   Hebrews 10:23-25; Acts 20:7; 1 Corinthians
11:18-34, 14:23-40, 16:1,2

OUTLINE

Discussion Questions & Thoughts

4. What should be the focus of TV/Radio ministry?
    a. If the minister visits you when you don't go to church, should you
    stay home more often so that you can get more visits?
5. Staying at home – praying, fasting, meditating on what is written in
    the Bible, is that the only thing GOD wants you to do?
6. Do you think GOD is in agreement with those that say, "I don't go
    to church, because there are too many hypocrites in the church?"

LESSON# 13   TOPIC: FASTING

READING: Isaiah 58; Matthew 6:16,18; Acts 10:30

OUTLINE

I. Fasting
Definition: Abstaining from food, or personal appetites, for a specific purpose, especially in times of crisis.
   A. Practiced by disciples of John the Baptist and the Pharisees. Mark 2:18
   B. Practiced by the Disciples of Christ. Acts 13:1-3; 14:23

II. Why Fast?
   A. As training for self-control (to be like Christ). 1 Corinthians 9:24-27; 11:1; Luke 4:1, 2
   B. Breaks yokes. Isaiah 58:6-12 (there's no specific amount indicated – two for this, three for that)
   C. To save a city. Jonah 3
   D. For direction from GOD, when in front of earthly authorities. Esther 4
   E. As preparation to cast out demons. Matthew 17:14-21; Mark 9:29
   F. To recommend and establish elders for a church. Acts 13:2, 3; 14:23
   G. As part of our service to GOD. Luke 2:37

III. How do we fast?
   A. Typical fast
      1. Abstain from food. Matthew 4:3 (but you can drink water)
         a. You can also perform a liquid-only fast.
   B. A partial fast: to fast a meal or certain foods. Daniel 10:3
      1. For some people, abstaining from coffee is a major ordeal, for others it may be sweets. Let the HOLY SPIRIT guide you.

LESSON# 13   TOPIC: FASTING
(continued)   Isaiah 58; Matthew 6:16,18; Acts 10:30

OUTLINE

C. The complete fast
   1. Abstain from food and drink. Acts 9:9; Esther 4:16
   2. A fast of various days can include abstaining from sex (with the permission of the spouse). 1 Corinthians 7:5

IV. When should we fast?
   A. When led by the HOLY SPIRIT. Romans 8:14; Matthew 4:1, 2
      1. Do you feel the need to enter into a fast? It is the HOLY SPIRIT that is leading you (for the flesh doesn't want this).
   B. When the Church is called to fast. Joel 1:16; 2:15-18

Discussion Questions & Thoughts

1. Does fasting cause GOD to answer you? No. Faith moves GOD.
2. Fasting is not easy. Where can I go for help in this area?
   a. Ask your Pastor & teachers for advice.
3. Every time I think about fasting, I get hungry! What's going on?

LESSON# 14   TOPIC: GIVING & RECEIVING
READING: 1 Corinthians 9; Hebrews7:1-17

OUTLINE

I. In the beginning - Cain and Abel. Genesis 4:3-5
   A. GOD respected Abel's offering (he gave the best of what he had),
      Cain just gave from what he had.
      1. Although not requested by GOD, the attitude towards giving
         can influence GOD.
   B. GOD delivers Israel.
      1. Egypt (representing the world system) detours us.
         a. GOD intervenes – through a man and delivers a nation.
            Exodus 3:7-10; 14:30, 31
      2. A covenant is given. Exodus 19:5, 6
      3. A covenant is ratified. Exodus 24:1-8
      4. An offering is received. Exodus 25:1, 2
   C. GOD provides for His ministers. Leviticus 8:31; Deuteronomy
      18:1-5; Nehemiah 10:37, 38
      1. The tithe under Moses. Leviticus 27:30-33

II. Israel asks for a king and the prophet reacts. 1 Samuel 8:6, 7
   A. Kings came to receive. 1 Samuel 8:11-18
      1. GOD provides a King. 2 Samuel 7:1-29; 1 Chronicles 22:14
         a. An inconceivable gift amount today. ($576 billion in
            gold!)
      2. GOD promises THE KING. Acts 2:25, 30
         a. What a combination - KING, PRIEST & PROPHET!
            Galatians 1:4, 2:20; Ephesians 5:25, Revelation 11:15,
            19:16

III. THE KING chooses HIS people: US! 1 Peter 2:9; Revelation 1:6
   A. GODS people give! Luke 6:38

LESSON# 14   TOPIC: GIVING & RECEIVING

(continued)   1 Corinthians 9; Hebrews7:1-17

OUTLINE

1. Tithe – Following the example of Abraham to the one without beginning or end. Genesis 14:18-20; Malachi 3:10; Hebrews 7:1-17
2. The Biblical order. 2 Corinthians 8:3-5
   a. The best. Malachi 1:14; Exodus 22:29, 30
   b. Give thankfully & joyfully. Psalms 27:6; 2 Corinthians 9:7
   c. Giving but not so as to be seen. Matthew 6:1-4
   d. According to your ability. 1 Corinthians 16:1, 2
   e. Following the example of the leaders. 1 Chronicles 29:3-9
   f. Liberally and joyfully. 2 Corinthians 9:6-15

Discussion Questions & Thoughts

1. How can we know where to give correctly? John 7:17, 18
2. When we give, is it to men or to GOD? Matthew 25:34-40
3. Who does GOD use to bless us, according to Luke 6:38?
4. Sometimes when an offering is taken, I feel guilty, and I give. Is that okay? NO! GOD loves a cheerful giver.
   a. An offering is a "Free will" gift. Whatever is in your heart or mind to give, give it cheerfully. The Tithe on the other hand is a requirement of faith. Why? If Abraham gave his tithe before the law, and he was the father of faith, then we of faith should also do the same. As Jesus said, in Matthew 23:23 "…these ought ye to have done, and not leave the other undone."

LESSON# 15   TOPIC: THE CHURCH

READING: Acts 2; Matthew 16:13-20

OUTLINE

I. The manifestation of the Church. Matthew 16:16-18
   A. There is only one church. 1 Corinthians 12:12
      1. A mystery revealed. Ephesians 1:3-10, 3:1-9
      2. Founded in Christ. 1 Corinthians 3:9-11
         a. PETROS & PETRA – stone & THE ROCK (Matthew 16:18)
      3. Baptized in the SPIRIT. Acts 2:1-4

II. Description of the Church
   A. Dispersed by persecution. Acts 8:1-4
   B. Renowned generally. Romans16:4
   C. Church (the Greek word is Ecclesia – assembly, gathering of believers). Romans16:5
      1. Body of Christ. 1 Corinthians 12:27, 28; Ephesians 5:22, 23

III. Our membership and relationship with GOD. 1 Corinthians 12:12-20, 27
   A. The Lord adds to the Church. John1:12, 13; Acts 2:41, 47
      1. Called Christians for the first time. Acts 11:26
      2. Called brethren. Acts 9:17, 21:20
      3. Christ is the head. Ephesians 5:23; Colossians 1:18-24
      4. Saved by Christ. Ephesians 5:25-29
      5. Built by Christ. Matthew 16:18
      6. Purchased by Christ. Acts 20:28
      7. Subject to Christ. Romans7:4
      8. Loved by Christ. Ephesians 5:25
      9. The bride of Christ. Ephesians 5:22-32, Revelation 21:2, 9

LESSON# 15	TOPIC: THE CHURCH
(continued)	Acts 2; Matthew 16:13-20

OUTLINE

Discussion Questions & Thoughts

1. The disciples would go to the temple to pray and not to the Church. Why? (We are the Church, but we meet in a physical place called the temple).
2. Every Christian is important in the body of Christ. Do you agree with this – and why? 1 Corinthians 12:12-20
3. Can you choose your function or position in the body of Christ? (Are you the head?) 1 Corinthians 12:28
4. How do you feel about your current position in the church?
5. Why do I have to go to church (temple)?
    a. That is where corporate prayer takes place, that is where we bring our Tithes and offerings to, that is where we encourage one another. Etc.
6. Can any person walk in to the White house, just to clean or mop a floor? Of course NOT. Only those that have been approved by security, by the President or staff, can have access to this physical place. How about access to ALMIGHTY GOD?

LESSON# 16   TOPIC: THE RETURN OF THE KING
READING: Genesis 12:1-3; 49:10; Psalms 2:7,8; Matthew 24

OUTLINE

I. The CHRIST'S (Messiah's) arrival is predicted at the beginning. Genesis 3:15
   A. The arrival is first for Israel, then to the Gentiles. Zechariah 9:9; Isaiah 45:22

II. The visible return encompasses two phases. Matthew 1:20-23; Luke 1:26-33
   A. The First phase is the unexpected arrival as a Servant (to Israel) and as a Lamb (to all the world). John 1:11, 12, 29, 36; Isaiah 53:3
      1. As a man He dies first (the Lamb of GOD), and then He's given His reward with the great. Isaiah 53:10-12
      2. The Church is established. Matthew 16:18; Acts 2:1-12; 10:1-48
         a. Now Jews & Gentiles can receive Him. Isaiah 9:2; Matthew 12:21; Luke 2:32; John 1:12, 13
   B. The Second phase is as Lord and King. Acts 1:9-11; 1 Thessalonians 4:13-18
      1. This also encompasses two small but important stages:
         a. <u>First Stage</u>: On way to the royal city (Jerusalem), the Groom's messenger calls the Church (Bride) to come to Him. John 14:1-3; also see 1Thessalonians 4:16; 1 Corinthians 15:51-58
            i. No one knows the day or the hour. Matthew 24:36
            ii. Signs are for The Bride. 1 Thessalonians 5:1-11
               a. As Noah's day. Matthew 24:37-47; Luke 21:34-36
               b. False Christ's arise. Luke 21:8
               c. Dangerous days and signs in heaven. Luke 21:8-11

LESSON# 16   TOPIC: THE RETURN OF THE KING

(continued)   Genesis 12:1-3; 49:10; Psalms 2:7,8; Matthew 24

OUTLINE

         d. The fig tree generation (Israel blooms in 1947). Matthew 24:33; Luke 21:29-33

       iii. A wedding? That's nice but the uninvited don't care. Matthew 25:6

       iv. Voice of archangel. 1 Thessalonians 4:15-17

       v. A great party. Matthew 22:1-10; Revelation 19:7

    b. <u>Second Stage</u>: The wedding has concluded and the King continues His journey to the city. Psalms 96:13; 98:9; 1 Peter 4:5; 1 Thessalonians 3:13

       i. He will be physically Visible as King and Lord, to the world. Zechariah 12:10; Matthew 24:27; Acts 1:11; Revelation 1:7

       ii. The arrival will be during a time of great trouble and affliction. Matt. 24:29, 30; 1 Thessalonians 5:1-6; 2:1-3; Revelation 19:1-9

       iii. The world has heard about the GOD of Israel and the Promised One. Matthew 24:14

       iv. There will be Signs in the sky. Luke 21:25-28

III. The return is to fulfill His Word, Are you ready? Matthew 24:44

    A. He will fulfill the promise to Israel & David. Daniel 7:13, 14; Matthew 24:30

    B. The Messiah will fulfill GOD'S promise to the world and to the Church. Matthew 25:6, 10; John 3:29

Discussion Questions & Thoughts

1. If He was coming in the next 10 seconds, would you be ready?
2. What if you've been sleeping, do you still have time to get ready?

LESSON# 17   TOPIC: THE NEW COVENANT

READING: Psalms 103; Genesis 12, 13; Hebrews 8, 9

OUTLINE

I. Two Covenants. Hebrews 8:13
    A. The Old Covenant (Sinai) – Physical and palpable
        1. Instituted in Sinai. Exodus 19:5
        2. Ratified by sacrifice. Exodus 24:6-8; Hebrews 9:16
        3. Did not invalidate the covenant with Abraham. Galatians 3:16-18
        4. Designed to lead us to Christ. Galatians 3:17-25
        5. Consisted in external rites. Hebrews 9:1-10
        6. Prefigured the Gospel. Hebrews 9:11-15
    B. The New Covenant (Gospel) – A Spiritual contract
        1. Promised in Eden. Genesis 3:15
        2. Proclaimed to Abraham. Genesis 12:3
        3. Prophesied & fulfilled in Christ. Luke 1:68-79
        5. Ratified by the Blood of Christ. Hebrews 9:11-23
        6. Remembered in Holy Communion. 1 Corinthians 11:25
        7. An eternal covenant. Hebrews 13:20

II. Two Existences
    A. The Physical existence is covered (Old Covenant - OC)
        1. OC – Written on tablets of stone. 2 Corinthians 3:7
    B. Our Spiritual existence transcends and surpasses the physical (New Covenant - NC)
        1. NC – Written in the Heart. 2 Corinthians 3:3; Hebrews 10:16
    C. Both covenants affect our existence
        1. OC – Dominates the physical. Romans 7:1; Galatians 3:10

LESSON# 17   TOPIC: THE NEW COVENANT
(continued)   Psalms 103; Genesis 12, 13; Hebrews 8, 9

OUTLINE

2. NC – Dominates our spiritual life. Romans 7:6
D. Both covenants are from GOD. 2 Corinthians 3:11
  1. OC – The physical law was glorious. 2 Corinthians 3:7
  2. NC – The spiritual law was more glorious. 2 Corinthians 3:8, 9
E. These covenants cannot be combined. Galatians 5:1-9
  1. OC – can dull the understanding. 2 Corinthians 3:14, 15
    a. This covenant must be followed to the letter by what we do, but can be discerned by the Spirit. 1 Corinthians 3:16, 17
  2. NC – Cannot be followed by what we do physically, it must be followed by faith, which is the spiritual. John 3:5, 6; Romans 7:6, 8:9, 14

III. Two Sanctuaries, Two Sacrifices
A. Old Covenant (OC) and New Covenant (NC). Hebrews 7:28; 8:1, 2
  1. OC – The physical tabernacles existed. Hebrews 9:1-5
  2. NC – This was a Tabernacle not made by physical human hands but also exists. Hebrews 9:11
  3. OC – Many Sacrifices. Hebrews 9:7-10
  4. NC – One Sacrifice. Hebrews 9:12-28

IV. Two Covenants of Blood. Hebrews 9:22, 28
A. Circumcision – the requirement for covenant with GOD.
  1. OC was physical - Genesis 17:11; Exodus 4:25, 26; Hebrews 9:22
  2. NC was spiritual – Romans 2:28, 29; 2 Corinthians 3:3
B. The legal requirement is fulfilled. Romans 6:23
  1. The Blood of Christ. Matthew 26:28; Mark 14:24; 1 Corinthians 11:25; 1 John 1:7

LESSON# 17   TOPIC: THE NEW COVENANT
(continued)   Psalms 103; Genesis 12, 13; Hebrews 8, 9

OUTLINE

B. Requirement fulfilled (continued)
1. The Blood of Christ.
    a. We now have fellowship. 1 Corinthians 10:16
    b. We are redeemed by the Blood. Ephesians 1:7; Colossians 1:14
    c. We are drawn close by the Blood. Ephesians 2:13
    d. This is a very serious Covenant. Jesus died in order to legally sign this covenant. Hebrews 10:29
2. Our Faith. Ephesians 2:8
    a. There is propitiation by Faith and not by sacrifices. Romans 3:25
    b. We are justified by Faith and not by what we do. Romans 3:25, 5:9
    c. We live our lives by Faith. Hebrews 10:38, 39; 2 Corinthians 5:7

V. Remembering the Covenant.
A. The new Covenant. Hebrews 8:13
1. The sacrifice by Christ is eternal. Hebrews 9:28
    a. Through Christ we have entrance to GODS covenant. John 14:6; 1 Corinthians 10:16, 17; 11:26-28

Discussion Questions & Thoughts

1. Would you sign any contract that's presented to you? Why?
2. Does a contract (covenant) indicate any responsibility between the various signers?
3. Do you thinks that a covenant signed in blood is important? Why?

LESSON# 18   TOPIC: THE RESURECTION OF THE DEAD
READING: Job 14:1,2, 11-14; Isaiah 25:8; Matthew 22:30-32

OUTLINE

I. Death – The consequence of sin. Romans 5:12
   A. Biblical words & expressions used to describe this event.
      1. Return to dust. Genesis 3:19
      2. Expire. Genesis 25:8; Acts 5:10
      3. Sleep. John11:11-14
      4. Depart. Philippians 1:23
      5. Separation from GOD. 2 Thessalonians 1:9
   B. This event is for all. Hebrews 9:27; Ecclesiastes 9:10
      1. Even at the rapture, the believer will go thru a process of transformation. 1 Corinthians 15:52

II. Resurrection s recorded iin the Scriptures. Isaiah 26:19; Daniel 12:2, 3, 13
   A. It was denied by the Sadducees. Matthew 22:23; Acts 23:6
   B. It was affirmed by Christ. Matthew 22:30, 31; John 5:28, 29; 6:39, 44
   C. Proclaimed by Paul. Acts 24:14, 15
   D. Realized or performed by:
      1. The power of Almighty GOD. Matthew 22:29, 30; 2 Corinthians 5:14
      2. Christ. John 5:28, 29; 1 Corinthians 15:12-56
      3. The HOLY SPIRIT. Romans 8:11

III. If a man dies, will he live again? John 11:25
   A. It is written. John11:24, 1 Corinthians 15:3, 4, 12, 13, 20
      1. All will resurrect. John 5:28, 29; Revelation 20:13
         a. Either for eternal death or eternal life
   B. The Believers resurrect. 1 Corinthians 15:51, 52; 1 Thessalonians 4: 13-17
      1. Incorruptible. 1 Corinthians 15:42, 54

LESSON# 18   TOPIC: THE RESURECTION OF THE DEAD
(continued)   Job 14:1,2, 11-14; Isaiah 25:8; Matthew 22:30-32

OUTLINE

III. If a man dies, will he live again? (continued)
    2. Glorious. 1 Corinthians 15:43
    3. Spiritual. 1 Corinthians 15:44
    4. We will be as the angels. Matthew 22:30
    5. As Christ. Philippians 3:21
   C. Without a doubt, we'll live again. Do you believe this? John 11:25-27; Job 19:25-27

Discussion Questions & Thoughts

1. Should you be afraid of death? NO! GOD has not given us a spirit of fear. 2 Timothy 1:7
2. If you are afraid, have you looked into the root cause for this? Typically, it's a lack of assurance of what awaits. If this is your case, don't be embarrassed; ask for the pastor to pray for you right away, it will restore your peace of mind. Also, memorize the following scripture in 1 John 3:14 "We know that we have passed from death unto life, because we love the brethren."

LESSON# 19	TOPIC: THE IMPOSITION OF HANDS
READING:	Exodus 29:10, 15, 19; Leviticus 4:15; 16:21; Acts 8:14-17

OUTLINE

I. The imposition of hands (also known as "The laying on of hands") was a custom of our Biblical forefathers.
    A. It was done when speaking a blessing. Genesis 48: 13-20
        1. They blessed with their words, and also by the laying-on of their hands.
    B. This was used to consecrate or dedicate to ministry. Numbers 8:10, 11
    C. Also used to transfer guilt. Leviticus 4:14, 15; Exodus 29:10, 15; Leviticus 24:10-14
        1. Because of this, you don't want just anyone to lay hands on you. You need to know who it is – either the pastor or elders of the church.
        2. This was a privilege of the ministry of the Church.
    D. This was often used to anoint and appoint a successor. Numbers 27:18-23
        1. This visible action imparted dignity, permission & authority.
    E. It was also used to impart capabilities. Deuteronomy 34:9
        1. The Spirit of Wisdom.
    F. This was also done to impart the authority of a prophet. 2 Kings 13:16, 17

II. Christians did this, but not quickly or lightly. 1 Timothy 5:22
    A. This was done to impart the baptism of the HOLY SPIRIT. Acts 8:14-17; 19:6
    B. For healing. Mark 16:15-18; Acts 28:8
    C. Signs & Wonders. Acts 5:12; 14:3
    D. Imparted gifts in the presbytery. 1 Timothy 4:14
    E. To send out missionaries. Acts 13:2, 3

LESSON# 19   TOPIC: THE IMPOSITION OF HANDS

READING: Exodus 29:10, 15, 19; Leviticus 4:15; 16:21; Acts
                                                                          8:14-17

OUTLINE

II. Christians did this, but not quickly or lightly (continued)
    F. This was done to ordain deacons. Acts 6:6

III. Jesus did this as He blessed the children. Matthew 19:13-15; Mark 10:16

Discussion Questions & Thoughts

1. With the possible exception of the laying on of hands for healing (following James 5:14 and Mark 16:18), if the Pastor or another guest minister places their hands on you, should you pay attention to what they have to say to you?
2. If you needed a spiritual gift, can you receive it by the laying-on of hands?

LESSON# 20	TOPIC: ETERNAL JUDGEMENT
READING:	Matthew 25; Mark 3:29; Judas 1:7

OUTLINE

I. Eternal Judgment has two phases (in the air and on the earth). Matthew 25:29-34, 41; 2 Corinthians 5:10
   A. First phase – begins with THE HOUSE OF GOD. 1 Peter 4:17
   B. Second phase – concludes with THE FINAL judgment. Revelation 20:11-15

II. The DAY of the Lord is extensive. It does NOT take place in one twenty four hour day. Revelation 1:7; 2 Peter 3:8, 10-12
   A. A DAY OF WRATH. Romans 2:1, 5-11
   B. A DAY of JUDGEMENT. 2 Peter 3:7
   C. Includes JUDGEMENT of the NATIONS. Matthew 25:31-33

III. This date is already decided. Acts 17:31
   A. It's for EVERYONE. Hebrews 9:27

IV. The consequences of that DAY.
   A. The JUST and UNJUST are separated. Matthew 13:36-43
   B. The perfect BALANCE of GOD will weigh. Proverbs 11:1
      1. Your WORKS. 1 Corinthians 3:11-15
      2. Your OBEDIENT FAITH. John 14:21; Galatians 5:6; Matthew 7:22, 23
      3. Your CONSCIENCE. Romans 2:12, 14-16
      4. The PERFECT LAW. 1 John 4:7, 8, 20; James 2:12
      5. The WORD of CHRIST. John 12:48
   C. The just in that day. 2 Timothy 4:8
   D. The DISOBEDIENT in that day. 2 Thessalonians 1:6-10

V. Are you ready?
   A. Don't wait - Get ready. 1 Thessalonians 5:1-9

LESSON# 20   TOPIC: ETERNAL JUDGEMENT
(continued)   Matthew 25; Mark 3:29; Judas 1:7

OUTLINE

V. Are you ready?
　　A. Don't wait - Get ready.
　　B. Warn the WICKED. 2 Corinthians 5:10, 11
　　C. Be careful that you don't DECEIVE YOURSELF. Matthew
　　　　7:21-27; Galatians 6:7, 8

Discussion Questions & Thoughts

1. When the Bible speaks of "The Day of The Lord," is it speaking about
　a particular 24 hour period?
2. If judgment begins with the house of GOD, why is it necessary for
　us to judge ourselves? 1 Corinthians 11:31, 32
3. What happens to us during the great judgment?

LESSON# 21   TOPIC: THE CHRISTIAN
                                        COMMANDMENT - LOVE

READING: Song of Songs; 1 Corinthians 13

OUTLINE

I. Let's examine the word we translate as LOVE (1 Corinthians 13, 14:1)
   as found in the Greek
   A. Eros – a pagan connotation of uncontrolled sexuality
      1. Animal, physical, sexual love. Although common in the
         Greek (especially for those days), it was mostly ignored in
         the Bible.
   B. Storge – rarely used in the Bible
      1. Love of family, of parents and children, grandparents and
         grandchildren, etc.
      2. It is found by negative inference (without natural affection)
         in Romans 1:31; 2 Timothy 3:3
   C. Philia
      1. Tender, friendly, brotherly and human
      2. Can be used to deceive. Genesis 4:8; Judges 9:1-5
   D. Agape
      1. The love of GOD – complete, solid, definite, divine,
         incorruptible. 1 John 3:1; 4:7, 8

II. The love of GOD. John 3:16, 17; Ephesians 1:6 (The Beloved)
    A. Without measure – represented the character of GOD.
       1. Omnipotent, omnipresent, omniscient & perfect GOD
    B. Represents GOD for GOD IS LOVE. 1 John 4:8

III. GODS love gives us access to unity with GOD. John 1:11, 12;
     14:23
     A. This love casts out fear. 1 John 4:18
     B. Reserves eternity for us. John 3:16, 17; 1 Corinthians 13:8
     C. Can do all things. 1 Corinthians 13:8
        1. In Christ. Philippians 4:13

LESSON# 21

(continued)

Song of Songs; 1 Corinthians 13

OUTLINE

D. Suffers long (can take it, resists to the end). James 4:7; 1
Corinthians 13:4-7

E. Stronger than death. 1 Corinthians 13:8; John 14:21; 8:51; 11:25;
Acts 2:22-24; 1 John 3:14; Romans 6:23, 8:37-39

IV. Love is the source of our Victory. 1 John 5:4; Galatians 5:6

Discussion Questions & Thoughts

1. Have you personally experienced the Love of GOD? How would you
describe this?
2. What does it mean that "perfect love casts out fear?" As found in 1
John 4:18
3. If you don't love your brother that you see, can you love the GOD
you cannot see?
4. Jesus said, "Love your enemies." How can we do this?
5. Can we really love the unlovable?

APPENDICES

READING: Psalms 18;28:1; Matthew 16:18; Luke 6:48

OUTLINE

I. Jesus – The Head of the Church. Ephesians 1:1-22, 23
- A. The Head is not: an Apostle, Prophet, Evangelist, Pastor or Teacher.
  - 1. These are described as gifts of the ascension of Christ. Ephesians 4:8, 11
    - a. What are the purposes of these gifts? The purpose is to equip and build up the saints (to perfect). Ephesians 4:12, 13
      - i. Perfection (completion) can bother us and hurt our egos (the "me or I").
      - ii. Our selfish desires can interfere with GOD"S work of perfecting us.

II. We are the <u>Body of Christ</u>. 1 Corinthians 12:12-27
- A. When we examine our physical body, we can better understand this concept.
  - 1. Can any part of your body decide it's not a part of your body?
  - 2. Is any part of your body superior to any other part? If this were so, get rid of the inferior parts & stay with the superior parts.
    - a. The function of the various members is different.
    - b. The Bible tells us that the members that are private are treated with more dignity than those that are visible and basking in the spotlight of attention.
    - c. Even members that we consider weak are necessary.

LESSON# A1   TOPIC: THE HEAD OF THE CHURCH

(continued)   Psalms 18;28:1; Matthew 16:18; Luke 6:48

OUTLINE

    3. As we examine ourselves, we note that our head causes everything to function properly, and that we exercise care for each of our members.
        a. Ever been sick? Noticed how all your body is affected? The head distributes this feeling to every member of the body, for it is one.
        b. For example – When you stub your little toe with the corner of some furnishing - your whole body is affected! See verse 25
  B. We are members of The Church of Christ.

III. Everything works well because of The Head – Jesus.
  A. You didn't decide where to place yourself in the body. Only GOD decides this. See verse 18
    1. Will you argue about the place in the body that GOD placed you? See verse 15, 16
      a. Remember in Genesis, "So GOD has said…"
      b. Even good desires don't necessarily come from GOD. See Matthew 16:22, 23
        i. Want to lead the song service but you can't carry a tune? Want to be a Teacher but don't know how to read? Want to be a Prophet, or an Evangelist – but it turns out that you are mute?
  B. Where have you been placed in the body?
    1. The law of witnesses - Deuteronomy 19:15; Matthew 18:16; 2 Corinthians 13:1

LESSON# A1   TOPIC: THE HEAD OF THE CHURCH

(continued)   Psalms 18;28:1; Matthew 16:18; Luke 6:48

OUTLINE

B. Where have you been placed in the body?
  1. The law of witnesses (continued)
    a. First Witness – The HOLY SPIRIT. Romans 8:14
      i. Even if you don't understand it, the HOLY SPIRIT is in you: the One that calls you and places you in the body of Jesus Christ.
    b. Second – the gifts of the Ascension. Ephesians 4:8, 11 for our benefit we will use <u>a simple definition of Perfecting</u> – *placed in the precise spot*
      i. When people are placed in unglamorous positions of service, I've heard some say "It's that the Pastor (or the Deacon or the Teacher) don't know what to do with me, so I'm placed out of the way etc." Think about this: Are you the head?
      ii. I've also heard, "I know more than they do." "I don't want to start there" Etc.
        a. You do know that this is actually the flesh?
    c. Third Witness – His Word. 2 Timothy 2:15
      i. Not satisfied with your current position in the Church? The HOLY SPIRIT has to prepare you first before you are moved to another level or given a different responsibility (in the meantime, don't allow your anxiety or bitterness to bind you. If you're cleaning the bathrooms, do it with joy and with ALL of your might. Thank GOD because He saved you and placed you in The Body of Christ. Don't analyze it. You're not the HEAD).
      ii. GOD rewards obedience. Philippians 2:8-11; Hebrews 13:17

LESSON# A1   TOPIC: THE HEAD OF THE CHURCH
(continued)   Psalms 18;28:1; Matthew 16:18; Luke 6:48

OUTLINE

    c. Third Witness – His Word (continued)
    2. JESUS – The HEAD: admires and respects those who submit to proper authority, and operate under that authority. Luke 7:6-9

Discussion Questions & Thoughts

1. Should we be submitted under proper authority in our Church?
2. What is proper authority at the church?
3. What is proper authority in the household? What about in: our jobs, our society?
4. When we look at our society, we can easily distinguish those that have the authority of the state. How do you know if someone is under proper authority (as pastor I try to request a letter of recommendation from other Christians that want to come and fellowship at our congregation. This usually helps my elder team know if these people can be trusted with responsibility even before they go through our classes).
5. In the world, we know where we've got authority. For example, you and I can't just walk into Buckingham or the White House to wash their dishes without approval beforehand. If only people at the church would know the boundaries set by GOD, they would ALSO operate this way!
6. If you're not under proper spiritual authority, you are deceived to think that GOD accepts your service.
7. Who is your pastor? Is it the TV minister, for you don't go to church? What a sad state you're in! Watching TV is NOT fellowship! In fact -you're NOT in the Kingdom of GOD. The Lord established His Church. It wasn't the TV. Don't allow Satan to deceive you anymore.

LESSON# A2	TOPIC: THE VISION OF THE CHURCH
READING:	Matthew 16:15-18; Acts 12:5; 13:1-3; 15:3

OUTLINE

I. Christ's vision for the Church. Habakkuk 2:2, 3; Matthew 16:18; Psalms 24:7, 9; Luke 21:28; Proverbs 29:18
    A. The mission of the disciples. Mark 16:15-18
        1. Here Jesus lets us know His Vision for the Church.
    B. The position of The Church. Matthew 16:18, Ephesians 5:22-32
        1. The Church is the Body of Christ. Colossians 1:18

II. A look at two early congregations – Jerusalem was established first and later on Antioch
    A. FIRST: The Jewish Church in Israel: Jerusalem. Acts 1:12-14
        1. The manifestation of The Spirit in the Church. Acts 2
            a. It all began with the Jews. Acts 1:8, 12
            b. We find here a proselyte from Antioch (Nicolas, one of the first deacons of the Church in Jerusalem). Acts 6:5
                i. The outreach to all the Jews begins. Acts 2:5, 8-11;
                ii. The Church was very comfortable and then Persecution began. Acts 8:1, 4
    B. SECOND: The Gentile Church in Syria: Antioch. Acts 11:19, 20
        1. The continuing plan of GOD. Acts 10:34, 35, 45; 11:18
            a. Christ reaches the Gentiles. Acts 11:20-26
                i. Many know about the Church in Jerusalem, but few have paid attention to the Church in Antioch. This is where the Church in Jerusalem sent the Apostle Barnabas, who was instrumental in the ministry of Paul and who also helped set him in the Church.

LESSON# A2   TOPIC: THE VISION OF THE CHURCH

(continued)   Hab. 2:2; Matthew 16:15-18; Acts 12:5; 13:1-3;
                                              15:3; Proverbs 29:18

OUTLINE

III. The model to emulate - The Church of Jerusalem and Antioch. As they were, we need to be:
  A. These congregations were composed of many members. 1 Corinthians 12:12, 14
    1. A Multi-cultural, multi-ethnic and multi-national congregation. Acts 2:5, 8-11, 38-41; 13:1
  B. The Church reaches out to the world. Mark 16:15
    1. An Apostolic and missionary church - impacting nations and establishing disciples. Acts 11:20
  C. The Church that is the salt of the world. Matthew 5:13
    1. Our congregations must be filled with people who are authors, directors, artists, musicians, businesspeople, teachers, doctors, lawyers, judges, governors, etc. John 3:1; Acts 8:9-13; 18:24, 26
  D. The Church that is led by THE SPIRIT. Romans 8:14
    1. With the GIFTS, FRUITS, and SIGNS and WONDERS. Acts 5:12, 1 Corinthians 12:1-11
    2. Prepared to reach the world. Acts 22:3
      a. Establishing schools, clinics, hospitals, etc. in the nations. 2 Timothy 2:15; Matthew 25:36; James 1:27
      b. Interceding at all hours for the community, the nation and the world. Acts 4:29-31
    3. As a family of believers, we reach out, encourage, and support other congregations around each other.
      a. We are THE BODY of Christ. Acts 15:22, 36

LESSON# A2   TOPIC: THE VISION OF THE CHURCH
(continued)   Hab. 2:2; Matthew 16:15-18; Acts 12:5; 13:1-3;
                                                    15:3; Proverbs 29:18

OUTLINE

  a. We are THE BODY of Christ. (Continued)
    i. Even if we have slightly different customs (the Church
       in Africa or the Caribbean might play much livelier
       music than one in Sweden but it is still the Church of
       Christ). Acts 15:3-6
    ii. Supporting missionary efforts. Acts 15:30-32
  4. Establishing churches throughout the world. Acts 9:31
  5. We are the exuberant and happy Church – with songs, praises,
     and dances. Acts 2:46, 47
  6. We are people congregating and fellowshipping together, our
     lives changed by GOD. Acts 4:34, 35
  7. We are a Church actively proclaiming the Gospel to the
     world. 1 Timothy 4:12

IV. We will meet Christ in the clouds. 1 Corinthians 15:51-55
  A. Led by the HOLY SPIRIT. Acts 8:39; Romans 8:14
  B. Holy and Anointed, full of the grace GOD. Acts 5:10, 11
  C. The Church formed in the image of Christ. Romans 8:29; 2
     Corinthians 3:18; Colossians 3:10
  D. The Church is the beautiful, holy, and spotless bride of Christ.
     Ephesians 5:22-32

LESSON# A2   TOPIC: THE VISION OF THE CHURCH

(continued)   Hab. 2:2; Matthew 16:15-18; Acts 12:5; 13:1-3;
15:3; Proverbs 29:18

OUTLINE

Discussion Questions & Thoughts

1. Are you part of the Church of Christ?
    a. If not, right now you can become part of it!
    b. Perhaps you've missed it when it comes to being part of a local church. If you'll allow GOD to set you in the congregation HE wants for you, you will enter into divine order, and HIS blessings will overtake you.
2. Can you be part of secular government, as a Christian?
    a. The Bible says *"not having mine own righteousness, which is of the law, but that which is thru the faith of Christ."* Philippians 3:9 and also we find that the Bible tells us *"Righteousness exalts a nation, but sin is reproach to any people"* Proverbs 14:34
    b. If you had any doubts, not only are you saved by faith (the gift of GOD) but by faith we are the righteousness of GOD! Our government needs us to bring them into line with GOD'S righteousness.
3. As the Bride of Christ, how should you prepare yourself?
4. If you're wealthy, can you still be part of the Church of Christ?

LESSON# A3   TOPIC: GODS ECONOMY

READING: Luke 11:9,10; Mark 4:26-32; 10:17-31, 46-52;
                                    11:22-26; 12:17

<u>OUTLINE</u>

I. In order to attain the success that GOD wants for us, we have to be
in the order that GOD has established for us.
   A. First – What is your current Position with GOD (where are you)?
   Galatians 2:20
      1. Adam and Eve "Where are you?" Come on, take responsibility
      and declare your position! Genesis 3:9; Joshua 24:15
         a. Are you obeying the Word? Ephesians 6:13, 14
            i. If so, your resistance will cause the devil to leave. Luke
            4:1-13, 18; James 4:7
   B. Second – What are you currently doing or what are you in the
   process of doing? Deuteronomy 11:26-28; 30:19
      1. Cain "Where is Abel?" Genesis 4:9
         a. You didn't like something in your life and you're still
         rebellious (some may call this aggressiveness)? Genesis
         4:7 Repent!
         b. If you're under GOD'S divine order, <u>you'll do what's
         right</u>. Hebrews 3:14; Philippians 4:8
   C. Third – What do you desire (what do you want)? Matthew 6:10;
   26:42
      1. Jesus asks "What do you want?" Mark 10:51
         a. Jesus does want you happy. John 16:24; Mark 11:24
         b. Are your desires lined up with His Word? James 4:3

II. The principle of "Sowing and Reaping." John10:10; Galatians 6:6, 7
   A. <u>Your position and works affect the harvest</u> you desire.
      1. Good works: Deuteronomy 28:8, 13
      2. Bad or dead works. Deuteronomy 28:38, 39; James 1:22, 25

LESSON# A3   TOPIC: GODS ECONOMY

(continued)   Luke 11:9,10; Mark 4:26-32; 10:17-31, 46-52;
                                              11:22-26; 12:17

OUTLINE

II. The principle of "Sowing & Reaping" (continued)
   B. Good seed: The WORD of GOD. Deuteronomy 28:1, 2; Matthew 13:19; Luke 8:11
   C. Bad seed: DESOBEDIENCE to THE WORD of GOD. Deuteronomy 28:15
   D. What will you choose? Galatians 5:16, 17
      1. Ultimately it boils down to Life or death. Deuteronomy 30:19; Galatians 5:19-26; 6:8
      2. If you wanted apples, what kind of seed must you sow?

III. If you sow to reap, you will reap what you sow. Galatians 5:6, 7; John 6:63, 68; Mark 11:24
   A. Sow Love. 1 Corinthians 13, John21:15
   B. Sow Companionship. Genesis 2:18; Proverbs 18:22, 24; Song of Songs 1:2-4, 8-10
   C. Conversation. Isaiah 1:18
   D. Peace. Romans5:1, John14:27
   E. Money. Proverbs 10:4, 5; 2 Thessalonians 3:10; Luke 6:38
   F. Careful! Some seeds bring destruction.
      1. Liars reap destruction. Revelation 21:8
      2. Violence reaps destruction. Proverbs 21:7
   G. Where are there seeds? Proverbs 18:21; Luke 8:11

IV. Sow in good ground & you'll reap well. Ezekiel 36:26; Genesis 18:14; Matthew 13:8, 23
   A. Don't get tired – there's a process of time required. Ecclesiastes 3:1-3; Galatians 6:9, 10
   B. The work GOD wants from us – to believe. John 6:27-29; Romans 10:8
      1. Sowing requires Faith and Patience. Psalms 126:5, 6; Hebrews 11:6; Malachi 3:8-12; Luke 6:38

LESSON# A3   TOPIC: GODS ECONOMY

(continued)   Luke 11:9,10; Mark 4:26-32; 10:17-31, 46-52;
                                                    11:22-26; 12:17

OUTLINE

  B. The work GOD wants from us (continued)
     2. GOD wants you to prosper. 3 John 2

Discussion Questions & Thoughts

1. You're part of the Church of Christ?
   a. What do you need in your economy?
2. To reap what you need, "What do you need to sow?"
   a. There are things (like healing, deliverance, etc.) that require us
      to have faith in what the Word says. For example, *"Is any among*
      you sick? Let him call for the elders of Church; and let them pray
      over him, anointing him with oil in the name of the Lord: and the
      prayer of faith shall save the sick, and the Lord shall raise him up;
      and if he has committed sins, they shall be forgiven him." James 5:14,
      15 (This requires that you believe in what is written, that you are
      part of a local church, and that you also believe that after the
      prayer you will get up.)
3. Does a good sower sow where they know they can't reap? No. If
   the ground is not capable of receiving the seed, the sower must first
   prepare the ground. If the ground were something like concrete, or
   steel, they wouldn't waste their seed, by throwing it there.
4. Do you have to give?

LESSON# A4   TOPIC: FAITHFULNESS

READING: Deuteronomy 7:9; Isaiah 53; Acts 6:8-15; 7

OUTLINE

I. Faithfulness (Adjective) – strict or thorough in the performance of duty, true to one's word, steady, reliable, loyal.
   A. For our purposes, we will treat this adjective as a verb – meaning, it requires us to do something to be faithful, and not for us to sit and wait passively like a piece of furniture.
   B. Faithfulness – an exact copy of something. 1 Corinthians 11:1

II. Various types of faithfulness
   A. The faithfulness of GOD. Deuteronomy 7:9; Psalms 117:2
      1. GOD is perfect. Matthew 5:48; Lamentations 3:22, 23
      2. The Word is perfect. Isaiah 55:11
         a. GOD is faithful to His Word. 1 Corinthians 1:18-20; Matthew 24:35; Psalms 33:4
         b. GOD hastens to perform HIS word. Jeremiah 1:12; Ezekiel 12:24
   B. Mans faithfulness
      1. Towards GOD. Isaiah 11:5 (The Messiah); Numbers 12:7(Moses); Job 1:1, 8; 2:9, 10
      2. Towards man. Jeremiah 35:14; Proverbs 11:13; 25:13
      3. The faithfulness of the saints in the Church. Colossians 1:2

III. Results of faithfulness. Psalms 31:23
   A. Man. Numbers 12:7; Proverbs13; 13:17; Psalms 19:7
   B. Faithfulness to what GOD gives you. Luke 19:17; 16:10
      1. Faithfulness is rewarded. Matthew 25:21; 1 Timothy 1:12
         a. Diligence is required. 1 Timothy 3:11, 2 Timothy 2:2
      2. Faithfulness has a reward. Revelation 2:10
   C. The faithfulness of Christ. Isaiah 53:12; Revelation 19:11

LESSON# A4   TOPIC: FAITHFULNESS

(continued)   Deuteronomy 7:9; Isaiah 53; Acts 6:8-15; 7

OUTLINE

IV. The consequences of our unfaithfulness. Luke 9:62, Revelation 2:10, 11
   A. Cowardice is our lack of trust in God (this is a lack of faithfulness). Revelation 21:7, 8

V. Examples of faithfulness. Job 19:25-27; Daniel 1:8; 3:13-18; 6:1-10

VI. Faithfulness of the Church. Ephesians 1:22, 23; 1 Corinthians 12:27
   A. Faithfulness is a requirement of GOD. Revelation 2:10, 11
      1. We need to be as Christ. Revelation 19:11; 1 Thessalonians 1:6

Discussion Questions & Thoughts

1. Should faithfulness be part of your daily life, as well as in the house of GOD?
2. Are we faithful to GOD if we are unfaithful to our church or to the people and leaders of our church?
3. Can the double minded man be faithful?
4. Can we lie to GOD and be faithful?
5. Can we lie to GOD'S people and still be faithful to God? Remember Ananias & Sapphira?
6. If GOD says something in His Word, are we being faithful if we ignore it?

LESSON# A5   TOPIC: THE ORDER OF GOD

READING: 1 Corinthians Chapter 5; 12:12-31

<u>OUTLINE</u>

I. Healthy organisms and strong structures require integrity (order, discipline, structure)
   A. Everything has a season (time). Ecclesiastes 3
   B. Families require order to properly function. Ephesians 6:1, 2; Colossians 3:20, 22, 23
   C. A healthy society requires order and structure
      1. Moses is advised in proper structure. Exodus 18:14-23
      2. Sports require order and structure. 2 Timothy 2:4, 5; 1 Peter 2:13, 14
   D. The body needs order and structure. 1 Corinthians 12:14, 19

II. The Church needs order and structure. 1 Corinthians 12:12-14
   A. Order and structure are necessary for us to have a healthy faith. Titus 1:13
      1. Proper order and structure will help us resist perverted or false teaching. Revelation 2:20
   B. Disorder must be corrected. 2 Thessalonians 3:6-15
   C. Removing whatever is evil. Matthew 18:8, 9; 1 Corinthians 5:3-5, 13

III. Order requires self-control and discipline. 1 Corinthians 14:40
   A. This must be done in meekness. Galatians 6:1
   B. In love. 2 Corinthians 2:4, 6-8
   C. Under submission to the pastors. Hebrews 13:17
   D. For edification. 2 Corinthians 10:8, 9

IV. As a ship, course corrections are necessary. James 3:4
   A. Discipline is required in words and teaching. James 5:12
      1. The Bible is necessary for correction. 2 Timothy 3:16, 17

LESSON# A5   TOPIC: THE ORDER OF GOD
(continued)   1 Corinthians Chapter 5; 12:12-31

OUTLINE

IV. As a ship, course corrections are necessary (continued)
    B. Corrections are required in our conduct. Psalms 37:23, 28; James 3:13; Hebrews 13:7
        1. Even in our congregations, correction is necessary. 1 Corinthians 5:1-8, 9-13; 6:9-11
    C. GOD is disciplined and requires order and structure in His house. 1 Corinthians 14:27-33, 40; Hebrews 12:6

V. Perfect order – imitating the success of GOD. Matthew 5:48
    A. Jesus was in proper order. Matthew 11:29
    B. The Apostles were in order. Acts 2:42-47; 1 Corinthians 11:1; Ephesians 5:1

Discussion Questions & Thoughts

1. Do we allow disorder in our own house?
2. Should we allow disorder in the house of GOD?
3. Is discipline designed to punish? Unfortunately that's how many people interpret the word discipline. Instead this word is dealing with order and structure. Discipline (structure) is so that everything works properly.
4. Would it be proper to say "Our walking in discipline is walking in proper order?"
5. What do you think of children acting out of order in school?
    a. How about children acting out of order in church?

LESSON# A6   TOPIC: RESPONSIBILITY OF THE CHURCH

READING: Romans 6; Galatians 5; Ephesians 4

OUTLINE

I. As the Body of CHRIST it is the Responsibility of the Church to obey the Head Shepherd and the under shepherds. John 14:15; 15:10
    A. We must obey what is written. Acts 5:29, 32; Romans 6:16, 17; Hebrews 5:9
       1. Then sin will not reign in us. Romans 6:12, 13
    B. We must renew the spirit of our mind. Ephesians 4:23
       1. Depart from disobedience. Galatians 3:1
       2. Depart from those thoughts that are displeasing to GOD.
       Philippians 4:8 "Finally my brethren, whatsoever things are true, whatsoever things are honest, whatsoever things are just, whatsoever things are pure, whatsoever things are lovely, whatsoever things are of good report; if there be any virtue, and if there be any praise, think on these things."
    C. We must put on the armor of light. Romans 13:12
    D. We must put on all the armor of GOD. Ephesians 6:11
    E. We must put on Christ. Romans 13:14
    F. We must also put on the new man. Ephesians 4:24; Colossians 3:10

II. The responsibility of the Pastors (Under shepherds)*
    A. Preach Christ. 1 Corinthians 1:23; Acts 8:5, 35; 10:36; 17:3
    B. Teach the Word. Matthew 28:20; 1 Timothy 3:2; 4:11; 2 Timothy 2:25
    C. Feed the flock. John 21:17; Acts 20:28; 1 Peter 5:2
    D. Prepare the body for the work of the ministry. Ephesians 4:12

All underlined sections of this lesson are excerpted from the book "First Principles, Rock Church of Virginia Beach"

LESSON# A6   TOPIC: RESPONSIBILITY OF THE CHURCH
(continued):   Romans 6; Galatians 5; Ephesians 4

OUTLINE

II. The responsibility of the Pastors (Under shepherds)*
   E. Spiritual watchmen over the flock:
      1. Protect against false teaching. Acts 20:28-30
      2. Discipline (place in order) individuals or body as whole. 1 Thessalonians 5:14
      3. Govern and lead people according to GOD'S Word
      4. As part of this responsibility, the pastors have drawn up the following guidelines as a means of knowing those who labor among us:
         a. Each person is expected to be faithfully and regularly attending services at Rock Church.
         b. Each person must have completed at least eight "First Principles" classes
         c. Must be baptized in water
         d. Must be filled with the Baptism of the HOLY SPIRIT, or actively seeking it.
         e. Is expected at all times, to have a good witness in their personal lives, such as:
            i. Dress conservatively (mini-skirts or suggestive clothing – are not considered appropriate for ambassadors of the kingdom). 2 Corinthians 5:20
            ii. Demonstrate self-control in all things. Ephesians 4:29

All underlined sections of this lesson are excerpted from the book "First Principles, Rock Church of Virginia Beach"

LESSON# A6   TOPIC: RESPONSIBILITY OF THE CHURCH

(continued)   Romans 6; Galatians 5; Ephesians 4

OUTLINE

e. Is expected at all times, to have a good witness in their personal lives, such as (continued)

    iii. Demonstrate qualities of leadership as ministers of Christ. 1 Timothy 3:2-13; Titus 1:5-9

    iv. Is asked to seek the Lord and be in good spirit and attitude when coming to minister to others.

III. The responsibility of the Church to the fathers & pastors in the faith. Matthew 15:14; 19:19; 1 Corinthians 1:3; Ephesians 6:1

A. There are fathers in the faith. 1 Corinthians 4:15-17; Ephesians 6:1; 2 Thessalonians 3:14, 15; Titus 3:1

    1. We must honor them. Ephesians 6:2-3; Colossians 3:20, 21; 1 Timothy 1:2; 2 Timothy 1:2; Titus 1:4; Philippians 2:29; 1 Thessalonians 5:12,13

B. We must work with our pastors in prayer and in our efforts to reach the world for Christ. Mark 16:15, 20; Romans 15:30

C. Monetary support. 1 Corinthians 9:6-14; Galatians 6:6; 1 Timothy 5:17, 18

D. Obey and submit to them. Hebrews 13:17

IV. The responsibility of all believers – to be under proper authority. Matthew 8:8-10; Luke 7:6-9

All underlined sections of this lesson are excerpted from the book "First Principles, Rock Church of Virginia Beach"

LESSON# A6   TOPIC: RESPONSIBILITY OF THE CHURCH
(continued)   Romans 6; Galatians 5; Ephesians 4

OUTLINE

Discussion Questions & Thoughts

1. Many people are not obedient to their pastors – are they in line with the Bible?
   a. Will the pastors have good reports for these people when they stand before GOD?
2. Are we faithful to GOD if we're unfaithful to the requirements of our local church and our leaders (of course we're not including those people and congregations that may be operating totally contrary to the written Word of GOD for they would not be considered part of the Church of Jesus Christ). Now, if there are some minor points of disagreements, this is not an excuse to be unfaithful! Instead it is an opportunity for meaningful study of the Bible.
3. What are some of the ways we can be out of order in the church?
4. Can a child grow up properly when people don't bother to correct or structure them?
5. The tithe was established to provide for what?
6. Should pastors be humble or poor? These two words are not about the same thing.
7. Should we consider old and retired ministers as disposable and useless in the Kingdom of GOD? Would you dispose of your elderly parents because they are old or retired? Of course not!

LESSON# A7	TOPIC: CONFIRMATION*
READING:	Acts 14; 15; Colossians 1

OUTLINE

Confirmation is a sacrament that was instituted by Christ through His disciples. Through confirmation, believers receive strength and become established in Jesus Christ. It is a time when those that have been faithful to attend and to submit to the teachings of a local assembly, receive both human and divine approval.

I. The definition of the word "confirmation" is: to make sure, to stabilize, to establish, to make firm, to render constant and unwavering

II. Was confirmation practiced by the Apostles? Yes!
    A. The Apostles confirmed their converts after their initial experiences with Christ.
    B. The Apostles confirmed after times of teaching. Acts 14:21, 22
    C. Confirmation includes being challenged and exhorted to go on in that which we have learned. Acts 15:32
    D. At times, they confirmed a whole church. Acts 15:40, 41

III. WHY IS CONFIRMATION NECESSARY?
    A. Prepares believers to stand during times of testing. Luke 8:13-15
    B. Grounds the believer against deception. Ephesians 4:14
    C. Motivates the believer to continually appropriate present-day truths in his life. 2 Peter 1:10, 12

NOTE: This complete lesson was excerpted from the book "First Principles, Rock Church of Virginia Beach" Used by permission.

LESSON# A7   TOPIC: CONFIRMATION*

READING: Acts 14; 15; Colossians 1

OUTLINE

IV. WHAT RESULTS WILL CONFIRMATION PRODUCE?
   A. Confirmation produces individuals whose hearts are established in faith and grace.
   B. Hearts established in holiness are free to love one another. 1 Thessalonians 3:12, 13
   C. Enrichment in all knowledge by Christ. 1 Corinthians 1:5, 6
   D. Walk worthily, with joy, through all. Colossians 1:10, 11
   E. The believer is equipped to live above reproach. Colossians 1:22, 23
   F. Makes believers thankful. Colossians 2:6, 7

Without confirmation, the church is weak. Young Christians must be established firmly in the truth, or they will become discouraged and often times fall. During times of testing, believers that can endure the chastening of the Lord are candidates to become mature sons of GOD.

This complete lesson was excerpted from the book "First Principles, Rock Church of Virginia Beach" Used by permission.

OUR COVENANT

By the grace of GOD, you have completed this series of teachings on establishing foundations, which will help you to fulfill all that is written in the HOLY SCRIPTURES by our GOD and Lord Jesus Christ.

Now we have the base to fulfill "the law and the prophets" as Jesus said. Now we can better understand how to live the Christian law: the law of love. "You shall love the Lord GOD with all your heart and soul and mind." And "You shall love your neighbor as yourself."

We complete our *"Foundational Studies"* with a commitment to each other and the Lord, that we will make effort to fulfill ALL that He has entrusted us, so that we may be found worthy of the rewards He' has promised us (of course we know that the use of the word "rewards" doesn't mean our Salvation, since that is His gracious gift to us).

As pastor of a local Rock Ministerial Fellowship (RMF) Church, I also include in our study series the book *"First Principles"* from ROCK CHURCH of Virginia Beach, which emphasizes important areas that we do not cover here. Nevertheless, because of the importance of the basic teachings we do cover, I have also included a slightly modified take-off of the "COVENANT OF CONFIRMATION" from the book *First Principles.* As Bishop John Gimenez would quote *Amos 3:3 "Can two walk together lest they be in agreement?"* to everyone of the Rock Ministerial Family, I also encourage our local congregation and all who will use these outlines, "Can two walk together ....?"

In the name of Jesus, "Let us now walk in agreement!"

COVENANT OF CONFIRMATION*

Ministry: *The ministry of LA ROCA Church (of course pastors can place the names of their congregations here), desire to make covenant with you as faithful members of this local assembly & the Body of Christ.*

Ministry: *Will you pledge to be faithful in your attendance of church services as stated in Hebrews 10:25? ("Not forsaking the assembling of ourselves together, as the manner of some is; but exhorting one another: and so much the more, as ye see the day approaching.")*

Class: I will.

Ministry: *Will you faithfully pray for this ministry and for this nation in accordance with 1 Timothy 2:1, 2 (I exhort therefore, that first of all, supplications, prayers, intercessions, and giving of thanks, be made for all men; for Kings, and for all that are in authority: that we may lead a quiet and peaceable life in all godliness and honesty.)*

Class: I will.

Ministry: *Will you conduct your life to the glory of GOD, patterning your life after Christ's, endeavoring to keep His commandments? John 14:16; 1 John 2:6: "If you love me, keep my commandments." "He that saith he abideth in Him ought himself also so to walk, even as He walked"*

Class: I will.

Ministry: *Will you be faithful in giving tithes and offerings as found in Malachi 3:10, so that there might be bread in the house of the Lord? (Bring ye all the tithes into the storehouse, that there may be meat in mine house, and prove Me now wherewith, saith the Lord of hosts, if I will not open you* the windows of heaven, and pour you out a blessing, that there shall not be room enough to receive it.)

Class: I will.

Ministry: *In turn, we, the ministry of this church, pledge to feed you as GOD'S flock according to 1 Peter 5:2, 3: "Feed the flock of GOD which is among you, taking the oversight thereof, not by constraint, but willingly: not for filthy lucre, but of a ready mind"*

And, we will watch over your souls so that we might be able to give a good account for your life here on earth as found in Hebrews 13:17: "Obey them that have the· rule over you, and submit yourselves: for they watch for your souls, as they that must give account, that they may do it with joy, and not with grief: for that is unprofitable for you."

*(Adapted from the book "<u>First Principles</u>, Rock Church of Virginia Beach")

REFERENCES

1. All quoted verses used in this book, are from the King James Version of 1990 by Thomas Nelson, Inc and the New King James Version by Thomas Nelson, Inc of 1994.
2. The Rock Church – "First Principles"
   When I spoke with Bishop John of the Rock Ministerial Family in late 2001 early 2002, to ask for his permission to incorporate a few short sections from their book First Principles (to studies that I had designed and begun to teach back in 1985), I commented to him "If I had known back in 1984 that your ministry had already developed study lessons on First Principles, I would possibly have avoided so many headaches when I started in the ministry!" (Well, of course I know and teach this, but I was looking for some sympathy, but Bishop emphasized to me that even if I had gotten these things, I would still have had to go through the process that every minister of GOD has to go through (as he put it – the necessary things) – and I know cannot avoid – so as to manifest the life and authority of Christ).

**Thank you Bishop John Gimenez, for permission to freely quote and incorporate a couple of very important sections from your book First Principles. As you requested, all the sections I have quoted and copied directly from the book "First Principles, *Rock Church of Virginia Beach*" I have noted and marked via an asterisk (*) at the heading and noted at the end of the sections, as well as printed them in "*underlined*" text. The Covenant of Confirmation is a complete excerpt (with some very minor modifications for use at our Church) and although not underlined (since it is a complete excerpt) an asterisk is also used and noted.

**NOTE: *Although Bishop John has gone to be with The Lord, this was something he asked me to do back in 2001, and which I continue to honor as if he was still in the present.*

CONCLUDING NOTE

Even as I mentioned in my introduction, there are areas where we Christians have differences of opinion. One of those areas involves the second return of Jesus. Another area where there are differences among us is the status of women in ministry (as you may have noticed, I have a strong opinion about this and I have briefly covered this in my introduction, along with my defense of this position).

Depending on your stance on the return of Jesus, you may decide that my OPINION seems to favor a "pre-tribulation" return of Christ (which happens to be my opinion). Rather than spend a lot of time as to why this is right or wrong, I prefer to leave this debate alone here. The purpose of these outlines is to bless and enable the local church and their leaders to move on in unity and not dissension.

As much as possible, I tried to choose a middle-ground in the outline format so that every pastor and Church can still accommodate their opinion (pre, mid, or post Tribulation) on this topic. I have no doubt that The Lord will return during dangerous times for the Church and quite definitely for the world. If He does come before the great Tribulation, as is MY OPINION, then I was right. If He comes in the middle of the tribulation, which is also my opinion, then I was still right. If He comes at the end of this period, which fits in with another of my opinions, then I was definitely right. You're possibly wondering how this is possible.

Well, I won't argue about the differences of opinions BUT I know where I'm ALWAYS right and that's aligning myself with the WORD of GOD. The Bible says <u>HE is coming again</u>! SO if it's before, during, or after, I'm right. HE is coming again! Now, the REAL QUESTION actually is, "Are you ready? "

ABOUT THE AUTHOR

Dr. Aramis Torres, along with his wife Rebecca G. Torres are Pastors and Founders of LA ROCA Church, in Sussex County, New Jersey.

Raised and educated in New York City, Dr. Torres found his "Rose of Spanish Harlem" in the Spanish Church "El Sinai." A year after their marriage, he and his wife purchased their first house in New Jersey. Four years later, Dr. Torres had an encounter with GOD that changed him forever, and set him on the path to Christian ministry.

In 1981, Dr. Torres founded the radio program "La Luz Guiante (The Guiding Light)," reaching a potential audience of millions of people in the greater Philadelphia and Atlantic City areas. It was during this time that the Lord and his local church directed him to establish a congregation in the city of New York.

As he and his wife were looking to move into a house further north, Dr. Torres and his wife began to encourage and establish a congregation of known families in the City, beginning with his mom who had gotten separated from her church. It was here that the congregation Calvary Christian Fellowship was born. After nine years as the Pastor, Dr. Torres took a leave of absence (sabbatical) so as to recuperate from injuries sustained in an automobile accident caused by a drunken driver. It was at this time that he and his family became members of "Love of Jesus Family Church" with Pastor Jason Álvarez, in Orange New Jersey.

In mid 2003, as Dr. Torres and his wife were visiting Pastor Luciano Padilla (Bay Ridge Christian Center of Brooklyn NY), the Lord moved Dr. Padilla, to speak to this couple and inform them that it was time for them to start a Spanish ministry where they lived. A few weeks later, as they were visiting Bishop John Gimenez of Rock Church of Virginia Beach, they were once again counseled to start a bilingual church in the area that they lived in. Shortly thereafter LA ROCA Church (Iglesia LA ROCA of Sussex County) was born.

In the process of establishing this congregation, Dr. Torres came to understand that it was now the time of GOD to take the studies that he had used for so many years, and publish them as a book. Without thinking too much about it, Dr. Torres translated his early outlines "Foundational Studies" into the Spanish version that was published as "Estudios Fundacionales."

This is a revisit of the same book published in Spanish (Estudios Fundacionales) but re-translated into English (as the original version of the 1980's was), and updated with a slightly longer introduction, expanding on Dr. Torres' stance on Women in ministry, as well as providing "prophetic" insight and comments about the "necessary" troubles that some of you as Christians are currently going through and that the rest of you will DEFINITELY be going through.

www.ingramcontent.com/pod-product-compliance
Lightning Source LLC
Chambersburg PA
CBHW020439290526
45785CB00002B/917